WHEN THE
LEVEE BREAKS

WHEN THE
LEVEE BREAKS

THE MAKING OF
LED ZEPPELIN IV

ANDY FYFE

Published by Unanimous Ltd
12 The Ivories, 6–8 Northampton Street, London N1 2HY
Tel: +44 (0)20 7359 2244
Fax: +44 (0)20 7359 1616
email: mail@mqpublications.com
website: www.mqpublications.com

A CIP catalogue record for this book is available from the British Library.

Series editor: Leanne Bryan

ISBN: 1 903318 56 4

Printed in Spain

1 2 3 4 5 6 7 8 9

Picture credits

Picture section page 1: © Herb Greene/Redferns. 2 top: © Chuck Boyd/Redferns; bottom: © Tony
Gale/Pictorial Press. 3: © Michael Ochs Archives/Redferns. 4 top left: © Barry Plummer; top right:
© Barry Plummer; bottom: © Globe Photos Inc. 5 top: © Neal Preston/CORBIS; bottom: © Neal
Preston/CORBIS. 6 top: © Rex Features; bottom © J. Thompson/Globe Photos, Inc. 7: © S. I. N./
CORBIS. 8 top: © Brian McCreeth/Rex Features; bottom: © Camera Press/Dave Wilson/PIX/NY.
9 top: © Mayer/Pictorial Press; bottom: © Camera Press/Heilemann. 10: © Hulton Deutsch
Collection/CORBIS. 11: © Rex Features.

Note: Every effort has been made to contact copyright holders; the editor would be pleased to hear from
any copyright holders not acknowledged above.

contents

Dedication

To Fiona, for all your love and the weekends I ruined.

Thanks

David Quantick, Mathew Priest, Danny Eccleston, Mark Blake, Lucian Randall, Kathy Ball, Chris Welch, Ritchie Yorke, Rich Robinson, John Reid, Debbie Bonham, Andrea at Trinifold, and, naturally, Rolf Harris.

introduction

"No one ever compared us to Black Sabbath
after this record."

John Paul Jones

In late 1970, Led Zeppelin were at a strange point in their career. Since forming over 18 months earlier, the band had recorded three groundbreaking, multimillion-selling albums, toured America six times, and become wealthy and infamous rock stars. And yet, no one outside their devoted fanbase knew it.

This was the conundrum: gods to their legion of fans, yet outside of that devoted army they were virtually unknown. Even though they had managed to turn rock music on its head in that year and a half, they could not get themselves taken seriously by the music cognoscenti: promoters in the United Kingdom didn't want to book them, their musical contemporaries were dismissive of their work, and the press, at best, attacked them for being a teeny rock act. At worst, it plain ignored them. In the United States, it was slightly different: at least promoters would book them.

Still, they could perform in front of 10,000 screaming American fans one night, then walk into a shop the next day and fail to attract attention for any reason other than their long hair. Other bands sold fewer albums and pulled smaller audiences, yet generated far more coverage in both the music and mainstream presses, and that stuck in Led Zeppelin's craw. This schizoid reality was starting to take its toll on the band members, fracturing them as human beings already pushed to a physical and mental breaking point by a grueling touring and recording schedule. No matter how hard they worked, no matter how far they pushed their musical boundaries, the band could not get the respect they believed they deserved. What could they do to get wider recognition and make their detractors sit up and take notice, make them admit that what Led Zeppelin was doing was worthy of their respect? There was only one route this hardest-working of groups could see out of their dilemma: work harder, stretch themselves further.

The result was Led Zeppelin's fourth album, a high-water mark not only for the band but for rock music as a whole. Never before, and seldom since, has a hard rock band reached such a creative pinnacle, creating a blueprint of such far-reaching consequence that it would inform all R & B–based music to follow. The Beatles and Bob Dylan had given music melody and a conscience in the 1960s, but in the 1970s Led Zeppelin gave it balls. With its fourth album, Led Zeppelin also helped to give rock music immortality.

With more than 22 million copies sold in the United States, Led Zeppelin's fourth album is recognized as the fourth biggest selling LP of all time, nestling in behind the Eagles' *Their Greatest Hits (1971–1975)* (27 million), Michael Jackson's *Thriller* (26 million), and *The Wall* by Pink Floyd (23 million). How many Led Zeppelin have sold of the album worldwide, however, is harder to gauge. The best industry guesses put the figure somewhere between a very conservative 32 million and a wildly optimistic 80 million. Even Led Zeppelin's official representatives, Trinifold Management, who still work with Robert Plant and Jimmy Page, are not sure how many copies of the album have been shifted around the globe, but they estimate sales at around 40 million. It's an extraordinary figure by anyone's reckoning, but it's only the most rudimentary measure of this album's phenomenal impact on modern music and the people who listen to it. Something always drags new generations of fans to Led Zeppelin. It's a love that once kindled, never dies, and nothing in Led Zeppelin's canon ignites the flame like its fourth album. Why? For starters, the record includes two of the most influential rock tracks of all time: "Stairway to Heaven" and "When the Levee Breaks." But there are the myths and legends of Led Zeppelin too, that here was the ultimate gang of road warriors marauding across the planet, belching thunderous fire and leaving smoldering ruins and sighing women in their wake. There are the rumors of Faustian pacts, wild excesses, and extreme behavior. The impression that these alleged deeds—not all of them untrue, as it turns out—could only be carried out by some kind of subhuman beasts merely made the band even more impossibly glamorous. No one— that's *no one*—has been more rock 'n' roll than Led Zeppelin. All over the world, since 1971, tens of millions of people have sat and listened to "Stairway to Heaven," attempting to decipher the lyrics on the inner sleeve and looking at the strange picture of the man with the sticks on his back on the album's cover. And as they did so they vicariously lived, through this band, the life of a modern-day Visigoth.

Led Zeppelin's fourth album itself is so "mystical," such a tablet of lore handed down through the generations, that its very name is debated among fans. Officially untitled by the band in the vain hope that critics wouldn't prejudge it, it is known variously as *Led Zeppelin IV*, *Zoso*, *Untitled*, and *Four Symbols*. It is even known as *The Stairway Album* by those not too bothered about exercising their brains. Whichever name fans choose to use (and for the purposes of this book, let's not be pedantic and agree to call it *Led Zeppelin IV*), they are bound together by an unforgettable experience. And that is one of the secrets of *Led Zeppelin IV's* success. No matter how many people buy it, no matter how many generations of kids "discover" it, *Led Zeppelin IV* still appears to all successive listeners as if they and only they have tapped into some secret society. Somehow, in spite of its vast sales, *Led Zeppelin IV* has managed to remain an "underground" album.

Rich Robinson, guitarist with the Black Crowes, doesn't actually remember the first time he heard *Led Zeppelin IV*. He was only three years old. His older brother Chris, the Black Crowes' singer, told him years later that a babysitter insisted on playing the album to them both, and such was the effect of the record on the elder Robinson that he "was freaked out for weeks afterwards. Really scared of the record, but strangely mesmerized by it, too."

Since that moment, *Led Zeppelin IV* became a part of his and his brother's life—but, unlike the rest of us, they actually got to *be* Led Zeppelin when they toured with Jimmy Page in 1999, playing a set of mostly Led Zeppelin songs. Page is now a firm friend of the family and Rich's kids call him Uncle Jimmy. But in the years between, Led Zeppelin became part of the fabric of the brothers' lives, just as it has become part of the fabric of most teenagers' lives for the past 30 years, particularly in the United States.

From *Fast Times at Ridgemont High* to *Wayne's World, Dazed and Confused,* and *Almost Famous,* films reference Led Zeppelin and, in particular, their fourth album, as a shorthand for all that is teenaged and stoned. The album is everyone's secret—sometimes guilty—pleasure, something "far out" that allows the individual to be part of an inner sanctum, one of a secret society. What's the one phrase from *Wayne's World* that people remember the most? "Stairway denied!" (when Wayne wants to test out a new guitar but is banned from playing "Stairway to Heaven.") Even though the use of the song in *Wayne's World* was largely ironic, it still hit a universal chord, and it was the only song the film's creator, Mike Myers, could have used as shorthand to demonstrate his point.

Led Zeppelin was also the first modern rock band. Conceived at a time when the first wave of British Invasion groups—the Beatles, the Rolling Stones, Eric Clapton's Cream, the Animals, the Who, the Kinks, and even Herman's Hermits—were either splitting up or hitting their artistic straps, Led Zeppelin was something entirely new. After years as a studio session musician, Jimmy Page had observed countless other groups argue and bicker, split up, reform, and split up again. After his experience in the Yardbirds, one of the era's most innovative and underrated bands, he was determined not to let the same things happen to his new band. There would be no arguments about musical direction (he was the boss, but "feel free to contribute"), there would be no arguments about money (there was plenty for everybody), there were to be no fights over "the ladies" (there were, indeed, plenty for everybody). His band was going to be louder, more streamlined, and more honed than any other before, and they were going to be the blueprint for everyone who tried to follow them.

Although Led Zeppelin came together at the end of 1968, they didn't come of age until 1971. With *Led Zeppelin IV*, they proclaimed their eminence as a new band for a new decade. Even now they are firmly rooted as a concept from the 1970s, lasting almost as long as the decade itself. And *Led Zeppelin IV* is a more 1970s album than any other, save maybe the Eagles' *Hotel California*. Put any of Led Zeppelin's first four albums up against those of their contemporaries and few can stand the comparison. In the space of three years, they not only invented heavy metal, but left the genre's other leading lights groping blindly in their wake as they pushed open musical and studio frontiers. And everything they achieved on vinyl was matched by a swagger and way of doing business that has become a blueprint for successive generations. No one would ever make a claim that Led Zeppelin was in it just for the art, but the money that came the band's way was a secondary concern to most of them. That they became so rich off their talents is in no small part due to the wiles and tenacity of their manager, Peter Grant.

More than anything else, what Grant did for Led Zeppelin was give the band space to create, both by ensuring them freedom from interference by their record company and by watching their backs at all times, physically if necessary. Compared to the earlier generation of rock bands—who had to find their own way and who were often ripped off or sold down the river in the process—Led Zeppelin was a sleek, chromed missile fired into the heart of the music industry. The combination of Grant and Page's huge knowledge of the music industry, the wide-eyed optimism of Plant's hippy ideals, and the band's natural talent for making adversity work in its favor, resulted in a reinvention of a music industry that the Beatles had themselves reinvented nearly a decade earlier.

No artists had such control over their music as Led Zeppelin did. No one before or since (and these two things may not be unrelated) generated more money for the industry: their final studio album, 1979's *In Through the Out Door*, single-handedly saved the American recording industry from one of its worst sales years ever. As record buyers deserted a music industry in thrall to the disco dollar, it was a rock album that brought them back into the stores.

Something gave Led Zeppelin an edge that allowed the band, as people as well as musicians, to stretch further than most others of the time. Some claim that edge came from a pact with the Devil, signed by three of the members, which would come home to roost as bad luck and tragedy dogged them in later life. Even some of their closest associates in the 1970s don't entirely discount the idea, so thick was the cloak of privacy and disinformation that these extraordinary men built around themselves. That suggestion is at the very heart of the band, never more so than on the fourth album. There is something inherently dark and dangerous about *Led Zeppelin IV*, something uneasy and unsavory that is tantalizingly offered, then pulled away from the listener time and again throughout its eight tracks. The tension it creates and the emotional turmoil it evokes are very powerful forces to those of a certain age. Unlike other such juvenile influences, the power of *Led Zeppelin IV* doesn't diminish over the years.

There is only one other cultural icon that has the same impact with those same kids of that same certain age: J.R.R. Tolkien's *The Lord of the Rings*. It is no little coincidence that *Led Zeppelin IV* draws deeply on Tolkien imagery. If you wanted to break it down into science, the equation would read something like this: *Led Zeppelin IV* plus *The Lord of the Rings* plus discovering girls and booze equals Very Powerful Teenage Male Experience.

Not everybody considered them gods, however. Nobody likes to grow old, and Led Zeppelin failed to appeal to an older generation who thought they "owned" music, the people who considered themselves the guardians of the counterculture. Led Zeppelin appealed to another generation of rock fans, the younger brothers and sisters of the self-appointed gatekeepers. This new generation had benefited from their older siblings' fight to change society and open up the world, make it less stifling, less uptight, but the back of the old rock order had been broken by political assassinations, the premature deaths of many of their contemporaries (Jimi Hendrix, Janis Joplin, Jim Morrison), the excess of Woodstock and the horror at Altamont. There was no going back to the "good old days" of postwar austerity and buttoned-down morality, however. This new generation needed new heroes. The Beatles, the Rolling Stones, Cream, the myriad West Coast and British Invasion bands, Bob Dylan—all were from a different era, an era that was drawing to a close.

In Cameron Crowe's film *Almost Famous*, real-life legendary 1970s rock journalist Lester Bangs is portrayed as telling a budding young writer that rock 'n' roll is dead: the true spirit has gone, the moneymen have moved in. To people like

Bangs, Led Zeppelin (whom he decried variously as "hyped, talentless nonentities," "lumbering sloths," and "emaciated fops") were more guilty than anyone of the heinous crime of making money from their art. But who was he kidding? The Beatles and the Stones were as rich as Croesus, and even Dylan, the generation's prophet, had squirreled away an amount of money his fans could only dream of. During the early 1970s, musicians were making more money than ever before. Crosby, Stills, Nash & Young generated more income than most; while David Crosby was on the phone to his drug dealer or sorting out a liver transplant, Neil Young would be on the phone to his realtor, buying more land for his buffalo herd to graze. Yet they never had to suffer the brick bats that were swung at Led Zeppelin for merely making money.

So what was Led Zeppelin's crime? Why were they singled out as traitors to the rock revolution when others were lauded? Part of it has to do with artistry versus commercial success. Here was a group of unknowns thrown together by a fading, albeit largely respected, pop star. Page, still in his early 20s, was a veteran of the U.K. rock scene, an innovator known to his fellow musicians but not particularly recognizable to the general public. As a session guitarist, he was the first person people called to play on studio records when the bands themselves couldn't cut it. There is even the suggestion that some of the greatest bands of the era had their guitarist's tracks rerecorded by Page, though the man himself has always been diplomatically evasive when asked exactly who made use of his services.

But in the end, recording for other people wasn't enough for Page. He needed a less restrained creative outlet. With the demise of the Yardbirds, it was time to put together a group like no other. Even before he found the other members, Page told Grant that the way they were going to do things would be different. Contracts would be signed only on their terms; if you didn't like it, you were the enemy. The band would retain control of everything it produced, and if you didn't like it, you were the enemy. To Page, U.K. promoters were already the enemy. When they didn't want to know about the New Yardbirds (Led Zeppelin's original name), the band simply packed up and went to America, where Page believed his talents were more appreciated and where he thought audiences were more open to the way he was stretching music, more willing to follow where he was going. Cue, from the gatekeepers of the music press, cries of hype and sellout. The British press didn't like the fact that this new band had abandoned their shores for the New World, even though all but a few of these same critics had initially ignored or, worse in the eyes of the group, criticized them. Ensconced in the United States, they annoyed people back home by achieving fame, fortune, and immense record sales without paying their dues, without keeping it real.

In a 1972 *Melody Maker* interview, Plant and John Paul Jones outlined just how deeply this criticism affected them. "Our egos have been hurt," Plant railed at the journalist. "For some reason, English critics have never told the truth about us. For some reason, they've been out to get us a bit. There's so much bullshit printed, it's just untrue."

Jones was more specific in his grievance: "We read pages on some band saying just how big they are in America. It's so annoying. Here we are slaving away, and getting consistently incredible reactions, and nobody back home can care anything about us. It's just not right. They say that Jethro Tull are brilliant on stage, well, they do the same bloody thing every night, the same gags, everything the same. Each of our gigs is treated differently, we don't have any set, religiously rehearsed thing. It makes the English press look ridiculous."

It's not hard to feel sympathetic. In December 1972, a year in which *Led Zeppelin IV* was one of the biggest selling albums and the band's previous three had all revisited the album charts, an article appeared in *Melody Maker* making predictions for the coming year. After suggesting that the leading new lights would be Pigsty Hill Light Orchestra, Keith Tippett Band, and Mighty Baby, it went on to claim that, "The great talent of Junior Campbell is really going to be recognized in the coming months, and Roy Young should get an increase in following. But bands like Led Zeppelin are going to have a struggle to survive next year."

Thirty years after the release of its fourth album, it's hard to believe that so little was thought of Led Zeppelin, and that the band viewed themselves as being under siege from all quarters except their fans. Even today, a suspicion of the media remains among the three surviving members. Each was asked to be interviewed for this book and each declined, partly because of their mistrust of the media, which they still view as leeching off their talents, partly because of this book's specific nature and their dislike of looking backward.

The world is more in love with Led Zeppelin now than it has ever been, and Page's, Plant's, and Jones's desire to only look forward is at the very core of the making of *Led Zeppelin IV*. For these musicians, questing for more was always uppermost in their minds, and that questing allowed them to write and record *Led Zeppelin IV*. Even if their subsequent albums, whether as a group or during their various solo careers, never quite scaled the same heights, Led Zeppelin never tired of trying.

Led Zeppelin's war with the media is hardly unique: all bands at some time feel the same way, and that outrage has its benefits, allowing them to maintain a gang mentality—their "us against the world" survival instinct—in an industry where every vicious little piranha will take the biggest bite it can. Today, enormously successful groups such as Limp Bizkit and Radiohead moan about criticism from journalists and pressures from their record companies. Both have received mountains of praise from the media but still snarl at it; both are only required to release an album every other year, yet they still feel they have to bite the record industry hand that feeds them. Now look at Led Zeppelin. Four albums in two years, virtually endless touring, and during all that time, having to put up with either genuine hatred or virtual indifference from most areas of the media. Led Zeppelin did have a torrid time proving themselves, but they got over it not by yelping about the nasty machine that wanted to beat them down. They got over it by becoming an even bigger machine.

And what underwrote that huge machine was *Led Zeppelin IV*. This album, more than any other of its time, changed the way people conceived, recorded, and sold music. It provided one of the greatest anthems ever in "Stairway to Heaven" (still the most played song on American AM radio, with an average of 4,000 airings annually), became a template for all rock music that followed, and was the inspiration for countless bands who formed in the subsequent years, from some that never made it out of the rehearsal room to others that went on to superstardom. Without *Led Zeppelin IV* there would be no Aerosmith, Kiss, Thin Lizzy, Iron Maiden, Van Halen, Guns N' Roses, Metallica, Red Hot Chili Peppers, Nirvana, Radiohead, Rage Against the Machine, Marilyn Manson, blink-182, or Eminem. Punk may still have happened, but even there, Led Zeppelin provided its protagonists with their biggest target, while the Sex Pistols' guitarist, Steve Jones, just wanted to be a guitar god like his hero, Jimmy Page. Even hip hop would sound weird without "When the Levee Breaks" to underpin its earliest days.

The making of this strange, compelling album, and its ramifications, is an extraordinary tale. Although thousands of groups have made millions of records since *Led Zeppelin IV*'s release in November 1971, few match its intensity or rival the story of the band that made it. This is not an exhaustive biography of Led Zeppelin—more of their heroic goonery over the years has been left out than included here. It is the aim of this book, rather, to show why this band—and its most popular album—have been essential to the fabric of rock 'n' roll music.

Look at those sales figures again. *Led Zeppelin IV* is the United States' fourth biggest-selling album of all time, qualifying as a "diamond" album (having sold over 10 million copies) twice over. In addition, four other Led Zeppelin albums have been certified diamond: *Led Zeppelin I* (10 million), *Led Zeppelin II* (12 million), *Houses of the Holy* (11 million), and *Physical Graffiti* (15 million). The band is, in terms of album sales, second only to the Beatles (163.5 million against 106.5 million). Even with these figures, it is possible to make a case that Led Zeppelin is actually the biggest-selling act of all time, as those overall sales figures take into account all albums, including live sets and compilations. Over the years, according to the exhaustive music Web-site *All Music Guide* (www.allmusic.com), the Beatles have been anthologized and repackaged nearly 80 times. Led Zeppelin, on the other hand, has cashed in on the compilation dollar fewer than 20 times, which strongly suggests that more people have bought the band's "official" studio albums than any other artist in history. That alone, without taking into account the huge cultural and musical impact the band has made, is enough to put them into what Cameron Crowe, in the sleeve notes to the 1990 *Led Zeppelin* boxed set, calls a "genre of one."

But all the huge sales figures and cultural impact wouldn't mean a thing if *Led Zeppelin IV* wasn't actually any good. How good is it? Just ask Dave Grohl, formerly of Nirvana and now of Foo Fighters, whose two unfulfilled ambitions in life are "to make it with two girls at once and drum with Led Zeppelin." Asked by Q magazine what his idea of heaven was, he replied: "A barbecue with a massive brisket, a keg on ice, surrounded by all of my favorite people. And *Led Zeppelin IV* pumping on the stereo."

your time is gonna come: before Led Zeppelin

At the very heart of Led Zeppelin lay any number of contradictions. Some of these were devised and planned by Jimmy Page before he even knew the lineup of his band, and some were the natural outcome of the combination of personalities. But wherever the pieces of the puzzle originated, they only added to making Led Zeppelin greater than the sum of its parts.

The central motif of the band is one that its members agreed on almost instinctively: light and dark, soft and hard, loud and quiet. Reflected in their music and in the personalities and backgrounds of the four musicians, it's something that gives them a complete balance: there are no gaps in either the combined genetic makeup of the band members or the metaphorical genetics of the band as an entity. Whichever way you slice through Led Zeppelin, you always end up with two members on each side of the divide.

First there are the affluent, middle-class boys from the south of England. John Paul Jones and Jimmy Page were both encouraged to explore music by their parents, who remained supportive even when their sons wanted to make it a career. That's a rarity today, let alone in the early 1960s. On the other side of the coin are the two working-class lads from the West Midlands, Robert Plant and John Bonham. They defied their families to live their dreams of being rock 'n' roll stars, escaping the gray mundanity of having to dig roads for a living for the rest of their lives. Page and Jones were artisans, honing their craft and taking it places it had never been before; Plant and Bonham were more visceral—they just had to get this noise out of their system.

Slice the band through the divisions of ambition, and you still get two people on each side. Page and Plant wanted the adulation, the love of the crowd and thrill and power of fame. Jones and Bonham were much more prosaic about their ambitions: they wanted to play great music and be recognized by their peers for what they did. For them, the trappings of fame were not a driving force, but merely a very fortuitous and pleasant by-product. For Bonham, the main reward for his effort and fame was a hedonistic lifestyle of Herculean proportions; for Jones, it meant a life of peace and security for his family.

John Paul Jones

John Paul Jones, originally John Baldwin, was born on January 3, 1946, into a showbiz family—his parents worked the variety theaters of the United Kingdom as a musical comedy act. His father, Joe Baldwin, was a pianist who had played with the Ambrose Orchestra during the Swing Era. When his son showed an interest in music, Baldwin tried to get him to play the saxophone, though his son was drawn to the electric bass, an instrument very much in its infancy. According to Jones, his father said he should play the saxophone so that he would never starve. "When he discovered I could play bass he just said, 'Well, good bass players are hard to come by,' and out we went together playing weddings and things."

During his early teenage years, Jones's musical education ran in tandem with his formal one, which included learning how to read and write music. Thus trained, he embarked on a career as a professional musician at 17, joining a band that had been put together by former Shadows members, Jet Harris and Tony Meehan. The Shadows had started as the backing group for "the British Elvis," Cliff Richard, before becoming recording artists in their own right. They went on to enjoy a string of instrumental hits in the early 1960s, such as "Apache" and "Kon Tiki." Meehan was also a freelance record producer for Decca, and there he used Jones as a session player. Developing musically, the youngster renewed his acquaintance with the organ, an instrument he had dabbled with as a schoolboy at his local church. "I even got into jazz organ for a while until I couldn't stand the musicians anymore and had to get back to rock 'n' roll."

However, getting session gigs in London was for the most part impossible for newcomers, and even with Meehan's patronage it took a lot of knocking on doors and auditioning until Jones's natural talent was accepted and regular employment came his way.

Rock 'n' roll was still a naive industry in Britain, and it consisted of a small, close-knit community centered on the old Tin Pan Alley in London's Soho district. Artists came and went. Largely expendable, they were often considered to be just "a face and a voice" to be packaged and sold for as long as the kids liked their smiles. There was precious little artistry. In many ways, the pop end of the business is run along similar lines today, with producers and songwriters putting together a package that can then be sold to the record company, and getting crack musicians in to look after the music. Session players were, as now, integral to the process, and they were regularly wheeled into studios to crank out production-line hits.

Even though there were plenty of songs being recorded and released, the early 1960s were not easy for a session bass player. On most records, the bass was buried in the background—a mere time-keeping instrument. It wasn't until the Motown sound, with its melodic bass beat, hit the charts in the middle of the decade that the instrument came of age and was finally recognized as an essential component of rock that could push along a melody rather than just add swing to the drums. Motown founder Berry Gordy, a jazz aficionado and songwriter/producer for Jackie Wilson and Smokey Robinson, decided around 1963 that it would be a great idea to put a pounding rhythm section alongside the blues and R & B that had been, until then, the domain of black artists. Having already had success with the blues-influenced pop of Martha & the Vandellas, Gordy cranked up the rhythm section of his house band, which was built around organ player Earl "The Chunk of Funk" Van Dyke and legendary bassist James Jamerson. The driving sound of that house band, affectionately dubbed the Funk Brothers, would appear on 22 number one pop hits in the United States throughout the 1960s.

As the bass became legitimized, Jones began to broaden his talents into arrangement, taking control of the sessions and working out the various parts the musicians were to play. His formal training was an oddity in rock circles at the time and, although arranging was a natural progression for someone of his multi-instrumentalist skills, even Jones himself has admitted it only came about through "panic." "I put me hand up," he once explained. "Somebody asked, 'Does anybody know how to do musical arrangements?' you say, 'Yeah,' and as the session gets closer you get a book and try and work out what goes where. After a couple of these situations, you find you're an arranger."

His breakthrough came with Donovan Leitch, the leading light of the British folk/poet movement and the man who was mercilessly goaded by Bob Dylan throughout D. A. Pennebaker's film *Don't Look Back*. Booked to play bass on Donovan's "Sunshine Superman" session, Jones stepped in as arranger when the original guy proved less than knowledgable. The single sold three million copies worldwide. Suddenly Jones was the hottest arranger in London, and his next arrangement, Donovan's follow-up single and signature tune "Mellow Yellow," sealed his status when it became a massive international hit.

The professional paths of John Paul Jones and Jimmy Page had to cross. Page was the brightest guitar talent on the session circuit; Jones, the rising new arranger. The musical circles of London in the mid-1960s were never huge. The coziness of the scene is vividly described in the autobiography of Eric Burdon, lead singer of the Animals. He claims that while at parties (and few went to as many as Burdon) he would walk through darkened rooms and trip over any one of the Beatles, Jimi Hendrix, Eric Clapton, Keith Richards, various members of the Who, or Ray Davies of the Kinks. In short, the hip social scene of the Swinging Sixties was hardly a diverse affair, and it largely fed off itself for its own amusement.

It's no surprise, then, that Jones and Page became acquainted and that, when booking musicians to play on another key Donovan track, "Hurdy Gurdy Man," Jones called on Page to play guitar. Later, Jones heard that Page was looking for a bass player for the New Yardbirds. By that time, both musicians had realized that working for other people was just too limiting. When Jones phoned Page in 1968, the guitarist was sitting in his home by the River Thames, 30 miles from central London, wondering what to do with his life.

Jimmy Page

For eight years, Jimmy Page had quietly been at the forefront of British music, playing as a session guitarist on (some estimate) up to 80 percent of the hit records of the day. He had also spent the previous two years as a member of the Yardbirds. The band had finally ground to a standstill while touring in America, and Page was weighing his options and contemplating his past.

James Patrick Page was born on January 8, 1944. His father was a personnel officer at an aircraft manufacturer and his mother had been a doctor's secretary. Both were from solid if unexceptional middle-class stock, and they lived a pleasant life in Epsom, a comfortable suburb on the southern outskirts of London.

Britain during Page's childhood was an anemic, drab place to live. World War II had drained the country's financial reserves and decimated a young male population only recently recovered from an even greater depletion during World War I. Food and gasoline rationing meant a restrictive and rather grey life for everyone, but it was especially hard on the young adult population, who only had to look toward the United States to see a much more glamorous, privileged, and open life. Little of this really affected the young Page who, according to his mother, was a "quiet, but fun" boy. He was an only child, and his parents were able to provide him with most of what was available in such an austere society, while summers were spent at his great uncle's manor house in the countryside near Northampton.

Page's musical interest, encouraged by his parents, began when he started listening to records and singing in the church choir. At 13 he was given a guitar and, according to his mother, "he just picked it up and started to play."

The only thing that got in the way of Page's music was school, where his guitar was confiscated on a daily basis. "I always thought the best thing about guitar was that they didn't teach it at school," Page has said. "Teaching myself to play was the most important part of my education."

Using his father as guarantor, Page purchased a second-hand 1949 Les Paul guitar and continued his bedroom education, working out the solos he heard played on records by Chuck Berry, Buddy Holly, and James Burton, Ricky Nelson's guitarist. In 1960, after finishing his exams, he was offered a job in a laboratory, but put regular employment to one side when he was invited to play guitar with Neil Christian & the Crusaders. Even though their son was still in school, Page's parents agreed to let him go on the road. The Crusaders are now remembered as a footnote to rock history only because of their involvement with Page and, later, with a young Ritchie Blackmore, who would go on to join Deep Purple.

They were, nevertheless, a big draw in their day and Page made decent money from the gigs. He invested his earnings well, plowing them back into his equipment, acquiring a foot pedal before most musicians had even heard of them. Loaded up with gear others could only dream of, Page became a trendsetter, leaving others to follow in his wake as he tried out every new invention and trick he could afford.

His reputation quickly built as word spread about this young hotshot. Session music inevitably followed. Every producer in London wanted to test his skills, and Page became known in studios and venues around the capital long before contemporaries such as Eric Clapton. Unlike John Paul Jones, Page never had to battle for gigs; producers came to him. Most British bands of the day played and recorded their own versions of American hits, often before the songs had been released in Britain by the original artists. On the live circuit, working bands such as the Crusaders played a mix of old rock 'n' roll favorites, more recent hits, and the occasional original track. In this way, Page learned to mimic others while developing his own style—a very attractive proposition for any producer.

Session work was lucrative, and no one would deny that Page had an eye for accumulating money. It became even more attractive to the fledgling guitarist when touring began to take a toll on his health. Never the most physically robust of figures, the fragile, stick-thin Page couldn't cope with the rigors of touring, sleeping in cold vans on top of amplifiers as the Crusaders traveled up and down the country through the night on to the next engagement. Still a teenager, Page didn't know how to look after himself properly, and he eventually collapsed with glandular fever. Bowing to his weakened constitution, he enrolled at an art college. For 18 months, Page's only real involvement with music was during Sunday jams with friends at his parents' house. His mother brewed tea for the gathered lads, among them Jeff Beck.

The jamming led to Page venturing on stage again, playing the occasional gig at the Marquee Club, often with Blues Incorporated, the band led by Alexis Korner. Alexis Korner was without doubt the daddy of British blues. The list of people who passed through his band in the the early 1960s reads like a *Who's Who* of U.K. R & B and rock aristocracy: those who didn't actually play in Blues Incorporated's fluid lineup at some point turned to its protagonist as a mentor.

The Marquee, at the time situated in the West End of London, was the premier blues venue of the day. Like the Whisky a Go Go in Los Angeles, it was the home of the local music scene, and newer bands would audition each Saturday morning to support the name acts later that night. Even the Who, the Kinks, and Jimi Hendrix were put through this process before getting a gig there. During his Marquee gigs, Page again attracted attention and was once again hired to wear the anonymous clothes of the session guitarist.

Other offers followed, thanks to young studio workers such as Glyn Johns, who later went on to become one of the most successful rock producers and engineers of the 1970s, working with Crosby, Stills & Nash, the Rolling Stones, the Who, Eric Clapton, and the Eagles, whose first two albums, *The Eagles* and *Desperado*, he produced. His younger brother, Andy, followed in his footsteps, getting his major break in coproducing *Led Zeppelin IV*.

Jimmy Page had to come to some decision: did he want to continue with art college or be a session hotshot? It wasn't a difficult choice. For the next four years, Jimmy Page ruled London's studios, played on hundreds of records, from "Baby Please Don't Go" by Them, featuring a young Van Morrison, to Joe Cocker's version of "With A Little Help From My Friends" and possibly—although Page is coy when asked and Ray Davies flatly denies the rumor—The Kinks' "You Really Got Me."

Eventually, however, grinding out tracks for the likes of Herman's Hermits began to pall. As other artists were totally changing the musical landscape, Page was being booked to play on muzak sessions. "It was stifling," he said of his final session days. "It should be stimulating working with other musicians, but it wasn't working out that way." Relief finally came when he traveled to see his old jamming pal Jeff Beck, who was then playing with the Yardbirds at a Cambridge University ball.

Undervalued at the time but now recognized as one of the innovators of British 1960s' R & B, the Yardbirds had been overshadowed by the Beatles, the Rolling Stones, and the Who for years. They were always seen as either too "bluesy" or too "pop" to receive their due credit. Put together by manager Giorgio Gomelsky as a new house band for the Crawdaddy Club when the Stones finally outgrew the seminal London venue, the Yardbirds' breakthrough came in March 1965 with their first U.K. Top 5 hit "For Your Love." Written by Graham Gouldman, later of 10cc, the song signaled the end for their star guitarist Eric Clapton. Gomelsky envisaged the Yardbirds as an experimental group, partly to distance them from the Stones. Clapton, however, was a blues purist who held little truck with commerciality. When he found out there wasn't even a musical part for him to play on "For Your Love," he left the group, which continued to move toward a more "pop" sound. Gomelsky immediately invited Page to join the band, but he declined. Clapton and Page were close friends, and the latter felt it would be going behind his mate's back to accept. Instead, Page suggested the then-unknown Jeff Beck and set in motion one of the great guitar dynasties of all time. Most bands are lucky if they can boast one true superstar musician, but over their relatively short lifespan the Yardbirds were blessed with three.

New boy Beck was an instant hit with the fans and the band's stock stayed high, with chart hits coming regularly. As a live band, however, it was a fragile lineup: Beck often couldn't perform because of excruciating headaches (possibly stress-related) that brought on short-lived bouts of mild depression. Friction within the group grew, and its founding members became disillusioned as bad decisions were made about which songs to record. The behavior of singer Keith Relf, an unstable character at the best of times, was also becoming ever more erratic in proportion to his increasing alcohol intake.

The situation came to a head during one particularly ramshackle gig at Cambridge University. An exceedingly "refreshed" Relf fell into the drum kit, and bass player Paul Samwell-Smith quit on the spot. Like Clapton, Samwell-Smith was a blues traditionalist for whom such behavior had become untenable. Luckily, Page had come to the show to watch his old friend Beck and, although he had declined the group's approaches for two years, he agreed to step in temporarily on bass. It just seemed to be the right time. He felt that his demoralizing session work was holding back his development as a musician. In addition, being in the band allowed him to play alongside his friend Beck.

Eventually Beck's increasingly unreliable health forced the group to shuffle their personnel. Page moved from bass to rhythm guitar, exchanging positions with Chris Dreja, making it possible for him to step straight in for Beck when he couldn't perform. With two such dynamic guitarists along-side each other, the Yardbirds truly flew for a brief period, and eyewitnesses to those gigs still claim them to be among the best live shows. But the band just wasn't big enough for two huge talents and, inevitably, egos got in the way of friendship. Beck cracked first, and Page gradually took over the band's musical direction as Relf and drummer Jim McCarty became ever more disillusioned.

At the same time, the Yardbirds had lost their way in the studio. Their record company, Epic, seemed unable to understand that they had an experimental blues act on their books, not a pop band. Mismatched in the studio with Mickie Most, one of the most successful British pop producers of the 1960s, they even recorded a whole album of material by other writers, *Little Games*, in an attempt to fashion as many singles as possible. The album was never released in Britain, and the fans soon began to forget the Yardbirds. Performing live in the States, meanwhile, their extended psychedelic blues jams were receiving rapturous reviews and audience response, making it all the more difficult to come to terms with their schizophrenic career.

It couldn't last. The final straw came when a horrendous live album, recorded under a producer better known for "easy listening" music, was shelved at the band's insistence. Briefly released by Epic several years later as *Live Yardbirds! Featuring Jimmy Page* to cash in on Led Zeppelin's success, it was almost instantly deleted when an injunction was slapped on the record company. The taste police alone should have prosecuted the company: this abomination of an album featured what Page called "bullfighting cheers" dubbed in after each solo and the sound of clinking cocktail glasses between songs.

After the final date of an American tour, Relf and McCarty left to record with Samwell-Smith. Dreja initially continued with Page. "My attitude was to try and see it through," Dreja told Led Zeppelin biographer Ritchie Yorke. "But there were destructive influences at work within the band. Eventually we all wanted different things so we just decided to can it."

Page also blamed these hidden conflicts within the group for its demise. "There were a lot of incidents that led to the final breakup, something that had been there long before I joined the group." Page, however, has never expanded on these dark words.

There was also the feeling that, just maybe, some things have a natural lifespan. The group had survived three major musical shifts, being pulled in different directions by all three of their high-profile and stylistically different guitarists. With Clapton, they had been the premier traditional blues act of their day. Beck took them along a different path with his melodic yet often formulaic playing. In Page, the musical magpie able to play anything from ersatz pop to the hardest

R & B and to mimic any of the great black bluesmen, they finally had a true visionary, albeit one who was, as yet, unable to take his fellow band members with him. Beck and Page all but took over the group's musical direction, challenging the vision of the original members. To Keith Relf and Paul Samwell-Smith, who both considered themselves British blues pioneers, being reduced to sidemen in their own band must have played havoc with their egos. Add in management changes and a record company that was both unsympathetic to the pressures within the band and unaware of that same group's strengths, and even a blind man could see the writing on the wall.

Robert Plant

As Jones was speculatively phoning Jimmy Page, Robert Plant was reaching the end of his apprenticeship playing with various bands around Birmingham and Wolverhampton in the British Midlands.

Born on August 20, 1948, Robert Anthony Plant had wanted nothing from the age of 15 but to be a singer, neglecting his education and dreaming of singing the blues. Although his parents were insistent that he find a career (they even set him up in a job training to be a chartered accountant), his teachers were less certain of his future, saying that he was intelligent but impossible to teach, as he wouldn't concentrate.

Although he didn't approve of his son's interest in music, Plant's father drove him to gigs and picked him up afterward, always hoping that the infatuation would pass. As Plant fell further in with an older crowd of musicians, the gulf between Plant, school, and his parents' ambitions for their son grew ever wider. "It was hard to combine school with what I really wanted to do," he explained of the rift with his parents. "At the time I thought the combination was great. Apart from being able to have a drink under age, it gave me a break into a different society with different values. I'm afraid it upset my parents a bit."

Plant put aside accountancy mere weeks into his career and returned to college to gain more qualifications, but at 16 he could barely go home because of the friction his long hair, if nothing else, was generating between him and his parents. Giving himself four years to make it as a musician ("It was the only time where I looked at my life from a long-term viewpoint," he said), he moved from band to band, trying to gain as much knowledge of the blues as he could. "The whole scene was enlightenment, a trip-out," he would recall 10 years later. "You can't give up something you believe in just because of financial reasons. Ten minutes in the music scene was equal to a hundred years outside of it."

But his parents couldn't see it, at least not until after their son was famous. Plant left home and joined the Crawling King Snakes. A more commercial band than he had been playing with previously, the King Snakes eventually ate their own tail, and Plant formed the Band of Joy. His new band was influenced by his early love for Sonny Boy Williamson, Tommy McClellan, and, when he hit the big time, Steve Winwood, a fellow Midlands singer who proved to Plant and others that you could be white and sing the blues. Just as the Band of Joy's reputation was starting to flower, however, its manager fired Plant, telling the youngster he couldn't sing. A second version of the Band of Joy was formed—strangely, still managed by the man who had just sacked Plant—but that, too, went to the wall. Plant gathered the final incarnation of his group. Among the members was a young, extremely loud drummer called John Bonham.

An intriguing historical aside to the Band of Joy was that its roadie, one Noddy Holder, would later form Slade, and suggest to his cohorts that Plant be asked to join them. Although largely unknown in the United States, Slade went on to be one of the loudest and biggest glam acts in the United Kingdom, notching up 11 Top 5 hits between 1971 and 1974. They eventually had two U.S. Top 20 hits in the mid-1980s, but today they are best remembered for Quiet Riot's cover of their "Cum On Feel the Noize," a number 1 hit in 1983. Ironically, considering that Slade was to become the epitome of glam rock's more outré flashiness, the other members blackballed Plant because he was "just too damn flamboyant."

As this third and final version of the Band of Joy flourished and grew, so did the friendship between Plant and Bonham. The group recorded three singles over the next two years and built a strong local reputation. They never managed to push past that regional barrier, however, and in 1967 they ground to a halt. At one of their last gigs, at the Marquee, Plant was watched by Alexis Korner, the man with whom Page used to occasionally jam on the same stage. When the Band of Joy finally disbanded, Korner got in touch with Plant and arranged for them to play a few dates around Birmingham, at the same time recommending the imposing blond singer to his London taste-maker mates.

Living off his future wife Maureen, Plant traveled back and forth from the Midlands to London, trying to get his career going. Demos were recorded, other musical pairings were made, but nothing gelled. Throughout 1968 Plant wondered where to go next. Then, while singing in a band with the rather terrible name of Hobstweedle, at a bland teacher training college near Birmingham, in walked Jimmy Page and his manager, Peter Grant. They had been sent to see—in Page's words—this "big, rug-headed kern" on the recommendations of Korner and another mutual friend, Tony Secunda.

Secunda, a producer and manager who would later guide Marc Bolan to international stardom, had tried to help Plant find a deal for years. Busy managing to hold Procol Harum and the Move together, Secunda heard the Yardbirds were looking for a singer. "I didn't think much of Keith Relf, had always thought he was weak, had no stage presence. The Yardbirds lacked vocal balls and I figured they could use Robert," he said.

Although they were impressed, Page and Grant were non-committal about Plant after watching Hobstweedle crash through its set of cover versions of songs by West Coast bands such as Moby Grape and Buffalo Springfield. Page had played on the same bills as these bands while touring the States with the Yardbirds and had never rated them highly. Even though his own band was best known as a live act that played swirling, free-form blues jams, Plant's choices were too psychedelic and lightweight for Page.

Within the week, however, he was in contact with Plant, inviting him down to London to talk. Ringing Alexis Korner for advice, Plant was told in no uncertain terms by the older musician to get his hippie ass down to London and grab the opportunity.

John Bonham

Following the demise of the Band of Joy, Bonham was still hammering away in long-forgotten bands and taking laboring jobs in an attempt to make ends meet.

Born in Redditch on May 31, 1948, John Henry "Bonzo" Bonham had felt the need to hit things since he was five, and there was little else he could think about—even in the mid-1960s, when he had very few prospects. "I used to play on a bath salts container with wires on the bottom and a round coffee tin with a loose wire attached to get a snare sound," he said of his first forays into percussion. "I felt nothing for any other instrument."

Although Bonham's parents tried hard to ignore the endless thumping, they eventually relented and bought him a snare for his tenth birthday. Nothing could have made him happier. Four years later he progressed to his first full kit, a rusty old heap of junk that was also bought by his parents. At the age of 16, while still wearing the purple jackets with velvet lapels that were the trademark of his first band, Terry Webb and the Spiders (lucky Terry got to wear the full gold lamé outfit), Bonham met his future wife, Pat. Married a year later, he swore to his new bride that he would give up the musician's life for her, but he still felt the need to play every night at home, which was a wretched 15-foot trailer. Having quit smoking just to pay the rent, they both came to the decision that the only way for him to make a living and be happy was by doing what he was good at: drumming.

Self-taught to read music from an early age, Bonham let his knowledge lapse and became much more of a "feel" player. Initially influenced by the same people as every other young rock drummer in Britain at the time, Bonham became increasingly interested in developing his own style. He felt more affinity with Booker T & the MG's drummer Al Jackson, Jr., (as John Paul Jones had felt with Motown bassist James Jamerson) than he did with the British Beat groups. "I've never been into using cymbals overmuch," he commented on his own style. "I use them to crash in and out of solos, but to me, drums sound better than cymbals."

Renewing an acquaintance with Plant, Bonham joined his band the Crawling King Snakes, but there often wasn't enough gas money to travel all the way to pick him up and still get to their frequent gigs. The transport problems proved too great, and Bonham left to join another group, A Way of Life, in which he developed his Midlands reputation for being the loudest, heaviest player in the country. Bonham took to lining his kick drum with aluminum foil to give it even more bang, and many clubs refused to book the band purely because its drummer was too loud.

Bonham got a regular gig with Plant's revamped Band of Joy, and for the next few years he earned enough money to contribute to the band's gasoline bill.

As the group's popularity dipped, they were offered a tour support slot with Greenwich Village singer-songwriter Tim Rose, who would later remember the impressive young drummer and invite him onto the drum stool of his backing band. It was here that Plant would track Bonham down in late 1968 to try to convince his old friend to join him in a new venture with a genuine rock star—who was now backed by a formidable manager.

Peter Grant

Led Zeppelin's manager was to be Peter Grant. Born in south London in 1935, he was raised by his mother, a single parent who had registered no father's name on her son's birth certificate. South London, and in particular the Battersea suburb where he grew up, has never been a "good" neighborhood: until the 1990s it had always been poorer and less advantaged than the far more fashionable suburbs of Chelsea or Fulham just across the River Thames. There were few prospects for someone of Grant's background, and the boy's chances were made ever more slender after his education was disrupted by World War II, during which the young lad was evacuated to the countryside along with thousands of other children as London was subjected to nightly bombing raids. It did provide him with a different understanding of the world, however, as he and his fellow evacuees constantly fought against local children who hated, in Grant's own words, "the scum who had arrived from Battersea."

Moving after the war to Croydon, a satellite town south of London, Grant determined to make something of himself, and at age 13 he took up work as a stagehand at a cinema/theatre. Smitten by showbiz, Grant carried his passion into the army when he was called up for service at age 18. While there he worked as a stage manager, putting on shows for troops. Once demobilized, he drifted into work as a bouncer at the 2I's coffee shop in Soho, then the hub of all that amounted to youth culture in 1950s Britain. Owned, bizarrely, by two Australian professional wrestlers, the 2I's was where skiffle, the U.K.'s first genuine youth movement, flourished, and where virtually every British star of the early post-Elvis rock scene was discovered. Grant's size and capabilities impressed the owners, who still promoted wrestling matches, and they convinced Grant to don a mask and enter the ring. The knockabout entertainment style of the "sport" would later hold Grant in good stead as Led Zeppelin's major enforcer: hammy stares and a threat of extreme violence coaxed sizeable amounts of hard cash from more than a few reluctant rock promoters.

Grant still harbored a desire to be an actor, and throughout the 1950s and 1960s he was given bit parts in films and TV shows. Roles as a body double included filling in for Anthony Quinn in *The Guns of Navarone*. He even appeared as a cowboy in *The Benny Hill Show*. Although the money was good and the work was easy, it was hardly his ticket to stardom. He decided to buy a minibus, to transport variety acts around Britain, and he eventually moved into tour management for visiting rock 'n' roll acts including Chuck Berry, Eddie Cochran, and Bo Diddley. His new line of work brought him under the tutelage of Don Arden, then known in Britain as "the Al Capone of Pop," and the father of the future Sharon Osbourne. Arden would later manage Sharon's husband, Ozzy Osbourne. (Sharon asked her father in the late 1970s if she could take over her husband's management, and Arden refused. She sued him for the contract, won the case, and didn't speak to her father for nearly 15 years. Nice family, but ruthless.)

It was this varied experience that gave Grant both his business acumen and ability to handle "difficult" musicians and situations. He learned much of his craft during the street hustling that had got him where he was. Among the many stories he would tell wide-eyed companions was one about the time he divested an enraged and drunken Gene Vincent of a cocked and loaded pistol that the singer was waving around wildly, and another about the occasion he took out six Italian policemen who were hassling Little Richard.

Successful as he was as a tour manager, Grant was still lining other people's pockets. The big money went to the actual managers of the artists, and he wanted some of the action. Setting up RAK Music Management with producer Mickie Most, the man who used to work the coffee machine at the 2I's while Grant was working the door, he had initial success with a 1920s pastiche act called the New Vaudeville Band. Other acts followed, but it wasn't until he came into contact with the Yardbirds, produced by Most, that Grant's true style developed. As a tour manager he had often been mother hen to his charges, furnishing them with extra cash or sorting out their personal problems, of which there were many. Like those under his wing on the road, he saw the money going to others, and his deprived upbringing brought to the fore a natural displeasure when people didn't receive their due. As a manager, he resolved to change the situation to look after himself and his clients first, and damn everyone else. Bands such as the Animals had been huge in the States, at times even more so than the Beatles, but they were left virtually penniless because they had been ripped off or taken advantage of by almost everyone around them. Grant believed he could remedy the situation.

While looking for a harder-edged band that could play on U.S. radio, Grant was approached by Jimmy Page, recently installed as the Yardbirds' new guitarist. Page knew of Grant through the many sessions he had played for Most, and he explained that their previous two managers had failed to make the band a great deal of money even though they had been successful worldwide. Grant started joining the band on the road and inherited the Yardbirds—and all their problems—from now-legendary producer/manager Simon Napier-Bell (who would later work with, among others, Marc Bolan, Japan, and Wham!).

Richard Cole

In Peter Grant's employ was a roughneck ex-scaffolder from east London called Richard Cole. Born in 1945, Cole had found himself at age 21 as road manager for the Who. He worked Grant's acts around the United Kingdom and the United States and, as the Yardbirds' tour manager when they finally fell apart in the U.S., he was to be the natural choice to marshal Led Zeppelin's forays into the States.

The Yardbirds' split had been caused by Keith Relf's and Jim McCarty's announcement that they were leaving the band while on tour in the United States. Grant drew up a letter that effectively signed the band name over to Page. It was the final act that cemented the pair together, and when it came to Led Zeppelin, there was never any question who would hold the managerial reins.

out on the tiles: Led Zeppelin conquer the world

In 1968, the world was being turned on its head. Martin Luther King, Jr. and Robert Kennedy were both assassinated as the U.S. civil rights movement challenged middle-America's martini-fueled comfort. Stanley Kubrick's *2001: A Space Odyssey* was released as the first men orbited the moon in Apollo 8. Students were rioting in Paris and Mexico. The Tet Offensive, the most disastrous American campaign of the Vietnam War, set off violent demonstrations at the Democratic convention in Chicago. And, possibly most important to pop culture but at the time least noticed of all, Tom Wolfe wrote *The Electric Kool-Aid Acid Test*, introducing the burgeoning hippie counterculture to the world at large.

Having pushed open the musical horizon with *Sgt. Pepper's Lonely Hearts Club Band* the year before, the Beatles were expanding the horizons of people's minds with the White Album, while their evil twins, the Rolling Stones, released their landmark *Beggar's Banquet* album. Cream and Jimi Hendrix were both reaching the end of meaningful creativity, while soul music had stepped up a gear with Marvin Gaye's "I Heard It Through the Grapevine." Even the second-division British invasion bands—the Who, the Kinks, and the Animals—had reached a turning point, and were desperate to find ways of reinventing themselves to stay current in the increasingly psychedelic musical world. In the States the original wave of Haight-Ashbury's beautiful people had given way to something darker in the Doors. Even groups such as the Beach Boys, previously perceived as the very embodiment of a clean-living band you could take home to mother, were more than flirting with serious drugs, madness, and Charles Manson.

It was to the tune of this rebellious underground soundtrack that Jimmy Page contemplated his future and wondered how he could extend his playing with a band, moving it along a road he had started to travel with the Yardbirds before they ran out of gas. He could still trade on the Yardbirds' name, particularly in the United States, but in the United Kingdom it was a spent force. Besides, the one surviving original Yardbirds member, Chris Dreja, was about to give up music completely and become a photographer (he later took the photo that appears on the back cover of Led Zeppelin's debut album).

What Page needed was a group that could improvise along with him while exploring the dynamics of what the Yardbirds had started to explore on stage at least—light and shade, hard and soft—a dynamic that has been the building block of every major musical uprising since, from acid house and rave to grunge and especially such alternative rock acts as Pixies, Nirvana, and Radiohead. The only genre that wouldn't build on Page's vision would be punk, which was a reaction against what he had started.

With John Paul Jones already in the wings, Page waited for Robert Plant to take up his offer to visit and see if they would get on. Hearing Plant sing at the teacher training college, Page knew he had found the voice he needed. "It unnerved me just to listen," Page explained years later. "It still does, like a primeval wail." Page couldn't believe this caftaned banshee was struggling to earn a living on the outskirts of Birmingham. "I realized that, without a doubt, his voice was exceptional and very distinctive." So, if Plant hadn't made it yet, what was wrong with him?

When the struggling, penniless singer arrived on the guitar hero's luxurious doorstep, he was unsure what was supposed to happen next. Famously, while Page was out later in the day, Plant rifled through his record collection and pulled out a number of albums to play when the guitarist returned. Page was amazed to find that his future singer had selected the very albums he was going to play to Plant to illustrate where he was coming from: those of Muddy Waters, Larry Williams, Buddy Guy, Elvis Presley, the Incredible String Band, and, surprisingly, Joan Baez. (One of the folkstress's songs they played to each other was "Babe I'm Gonna Leave You," the second track on Led Zeppelin's debut album.) The only musical taste they didn't share was for the new Californian bands, of which Plant was so enamored.

"When Jimmy saw that I had picked out the same records, we just giggled at each other a bit," Plant later recalled. As Page outlined his plans and musical ideas, Plant couldn't believe what he was hearing. "I remember thinking to myself, 'It's so fresh. I don't know this person, but why not try it?'"

What Page wanted was a singer who could match his guitar playing, a vocalist who was as adept at abstract sound as he was at belting out psychedelic blues. This was all manna from heaven for Plant. Even in his earliest days as a budding singer, Plant had marveled at Robert Johnson's ability to make his voice complement his guitar playing, as if the primal bluesman considered his vocal cords to be the same as guitar strings.

The band was still minus a drummer. Plant suggested the only man he knew for the job, John Bonham, who was at the time playing in Oxford with Tim Rose. Hitchhiking to Oxford from Page's house, Plant tried to convince his buddy to return with him and join the New Yardbirds. However, for the first time in his life, Bonham was making proper money (£40 a week, or something in the region of $100) doing what he loved and he also had other offers from Joe Cocker and Chris Farlowe. Plant traveled back to London, convinced that Bonham was the man they needed. He took Page to see the drummer when Tim Rose came to London. At that time Page was still unsure whether or not to move along a softer path more in line with English folk groups such as Pentangle. After taking in Bonham's playing, however, he knew which way to go.

Though he was earning decent money for a drummer, Bonham was still unable to afford a phone. Plant and Peter Grant mounted a campaign to secure his services, sending something like 50 telegrams over the following weeks to his local pub, the Three Men in a Boat, in Walsall.

"It was baffling," Bonham recalled. "I thought the Yardbirds were finished, but I knew Jimmy was a good guitarist and Robert was a good singer. I thought, 'I've got nothing anyway, so anything is better than nothing,' and I liked their musical ideas the best."

Finally, the four musicians met in a small basement room in Gerrard Street, now famous as the heart of London's Chinatown. One run through the Yardbirds' "Train Kept A' Rollin'" and everything else was history. As Jones later recalled: "The whole room just exploded. There were lots of silly grins and 'oh, yeah, man, this is it, man, yeah.' It was pretty bloody obvious from the first number that this was going to work." Plant was even more excited by that first rehearsal. "I've never been so turned on in my life. Although we were all steeped in the blues and R & B, we found out in the first hour and a half that we had our own identity."

Though it was obvious that this was no mere New Yardbirds, the old band still had dates in Scandinavia to fulfill, and it was decided to use these as a testing ground for songs for the debut album. There was, however, one detail to be taken care of first. As they left that first rehearsal, pop star Page asked the others—two of them with barely a pound between them—to chip in for the beers. It wasn't long before his reputation as a skinflint became apparent to the others, who eventually nicknamed him "Led Wallet."

The Scandinavian tour only reinforced the band's feeling that a new name befitted this new beginning for all four of them. The accepted story of the group name's genesis is that Page remembered it from the sessions that produced "Beck's Bolero," the track that launched Jeff Beck as a solo artist after he left the Yardbirds. The sessions included Keith Moon and John Entwistle during one of their many disenchanted periods with the Who. After the session Moon had tried to convince Entwistle, Page, Beck, and keyboard player Nicky Hopkins that they should form a supergroup called Lead

Zeppelin, a corruption of the phrase "going down like a lead balloon," meaning to fail in front of an audience. Remembering the conversation a year later, Page suggested it to the rest of the group, who agreed it somehow captured their essence, the central idea of light and heavy.

Entwistle, however, remembered it differently. He claimed, in Ritchie Yorke's band biography, that the name was his idea for a band that he and Moon would form. During a chauffeured ride in New York he had hit on the name, and was overheard by the man driving them. That man, Richard Cole, was soon to become Peter Grant's assistant and later Led Zeppelin's notorious tour manager. Whatever the name's provenance, its ownership has never since been in dispute and, whether it was nicked or donated, fans the world over should be eternally grateful to the Who's rhythm section, as it saved them from buying albums by either Mad Dogs or the ever-so-hilarious Whoopee Cushion, two other options considered at the time. The final twist in the name's tale was dropping the "a." Concerned that promoters in America would pronounce "lead" to rhyme with speed, Peter Grant simply removed the offending ambiguous vowel.

Returning from Scandinavia, rehearsals began in earnest for Led Zeppelin's first album. Having already made a selection of possible songs, Page drilled the band and took them to a studio, recording the entire album in just 30 hours for £1,700 (around $4,000 back then). Armed with the demo tapes, Grant flew to America with the intention of securing a worldwide deal for an essentially unknown group whose accomplishments to date consisted of a handful of European gigs and a few meager weeks of rehearsals under their belt. Even for Grant, who, through his association with Led Zeppelin, would change the face of rock management over the next five years, this was a tall order.

Page and Grant fitted together perfectly. One was a talented musician who would do whatever his manager asked if it meant money and success, and the other was a manager whom the musician could trust without question—who was dedicated to the band, not the industry. Almost uniquely among managers of the time and very important to Page, Grant never interfered in the music, giving the act complete artistic freedom. Years later, the manager's wife complained that Grant loved Jimmy Page more than he loved her. She wasn't necessarily joking, either.

It was obvious to Grant that there was no point in trying to get a deal for Led Zeppelin in Britain. The only strong selling point he had was Page's attachment to the Yardbirds, a group that even one of his new charges, John Bonham, had thought was finished. In spite of relentless hustling, Grant couldn't work up any enthusiasm for his new act among the U.K. record companies and promoters. Those who did go and see them during a handful of early gigs complained that they were too loud and too self-indulgent with their guitar and drum solos, or that they just plain didn't get it.

Heading to the States, Grant went straight to Atlantic Records. Label founders Ahmet Ertegun and Jerry Wexler were mesmerized by the tapes he played to them. The band had already been recommended to Wexler by a most unlikely source, Dusty Springfield, who had used John Paul Jones as an arranger—a fact the record company man found very impressive. Relatively quick negotiations followed, and Grant left Atlantic with a handshake, an advance of $200,000 and a worldwide distribution deal.

Many factors of Led Zeppelin's signing were unusual. First, that amount of money for an unheard-of band was in itself unheard of. Also, Led Zeppelin was the first rock band ever signed directly to the legendary, but mainly soul- and jazz-oriented, label. All their other "alternative" acts—Cream, Buffalo Springfield, and Iron Butterfly—were signed to the subsidiary Atco label. More important than this vanity, however, was Grant's real coup: complete control for the artists over recording, artwork, promotion, and all business. Essentially, the roles Atlantic played in the band's career were initially those of bankroller and distributor, which later morphed into substantial bean counter. It was an unprecedented deal in 1968, and is still the exception rather than the norm today. Led Zeppelin didn't even have an A & R (Artist and Repertoire) man at the company, instead reporting directly to Ertegun and Wexler. Just how weighted the deal was in the band's favor would become apparent when it came to shaping *Led Zeppelin IV*.

Freshly triumphant from the Atlantic negotiating table, Grant couldn't resist one last piece of skullduggery. The Yardbirds had been signed to Epic Records, a subsidiary of Columbia. When Columbia heard that Jimmy Page was putting together a new band, they not unnaturally assumed the guitarist was still tied to their company. Having already secured his deal at Atlantic, Grant visited the head of Columbia, Clive Davis, purely out of a sense of mischief. Sitting with Davis, a man almost as legendary within the industry as Ahmet Ertegun, Grant led the conversation through every topic possible without making mention of Led Zeppelin. When Davis finally cracked and asked about Jimmy Page, Grant just said, "Oh no, we've already signed the Zeppelin to Atlantic." Davis, who had considered the Yardbirds one of his pet projects, went berserk, but he had to accept that Page had never been signed to his label as an individual, merely as part of the group.

It's safe to say that Grant left that office a very satisfied man: within a matter of days he had fronted out two of the biggest names in the entire music industry—Davis and Ertegun—and both times he left with the upper hand. Not bad for written-off "scum" from Battersea.

Led Zeppelin's debut album was released in January 1969, and it struck a chord with a young, mostly male audience desperate for straightforward, loud music, which is what the album is largely, yet unjustly, remembered for. From the second song, "Babe I'm Gonna Leave You," acoustic flourishes (remember, this was a traditional song most recently recorded by arch folk warbler Joan Baez) mix with driving blues rock, while the blasting "Communication Breakdown" and the cornerstone track "Dazed and Confused" allowed for heads-down, hair-shaking, no nonsense screaming and bedroom-mirror dreams of becoming a guitar god. The rapport between the four band members was obvious, and Led Zeppelin I is an astonishingly dynamic, aggressive, and focused debut album.

But Led Zeppelin wasn't all about power and volume. There was an ace up its sleeve: subtlety. Heavy metal was still a fledgling genre and, although it already had a basis in the hard, bass-heavy blues rock of Jimi Hendrix, Steppenwolf,

Blue Cheer, and Iron Butterfly, it was Led Zeppelin's debut that finally made it fly. The light and shade that Led Zeppelin brought to heavy rock had the same effect on the young genre that Nirvana's *Nevermind* had on grunge in 1991, showing others the way to create a dynamic new sound from something that could have quickly stagnated and become a mere musical footnote.

Few critics thought so at the time, however, and here began the sorry saga of Led Zeppelin's relationship with the music press. The media was wary of the band. The combination of its huge advance from Atlantic, its watertight contract, its lack of credentials, and its almost instantaneous live success added up to "hype" in the eyes of journalists who were totally hung up on "authenticity." *Rolling Stone* magazine panned the album, labeling the group as merely the combination of a guitar virtuoso, a competent rhythm section, and a pretty soul belter, the latest in a "long line" of British acts that ironically so far consisted only of Cream and the Jeff Beck Group. In the United Kingdom, few members of the media gave the album anything but a lukewarm response, criticizing its bludgeoning style and derivative blues.

Luckily for Peter Grant, the media didn't really form a part of his plans for breaking the group. His strategy—admittedly, a high-risk one—was to play the group into the hearts of its audience by touring relentlessly, and it paid off. The self-belief inside the Led Zeppelin camp somehow transferred to its audiences, and gradually, over two massive American tours, the band seeped into the consciousness of a new generation of rock 'n' roll fans who wanted their own heroes, not those of their elders. Few had more belief in the act than their tour manager, Richard Cole. Working for Grant, he had taken all his boss's acts on the road, but he finally asked Grant to let him work with just one: Led Zeppelin. "I said, 'Let me stay with one fucking band instead of jumping about.' I wanted some of the glory because I knew they were going to make money, I knew they were going to be monsters," said Cole.

For the next two years the road would be Led Zeppelin's natural habitat. For the band, it was just common sense to tour heavily, especially in America, which they would travel across an incredible six times within those 24 months. To promote their album they conducted two U.S. tours in quick succession, which were separated by a short string of U.K. club dates. The strategy worked, and by the end of February *Led Zeppelin I* was at number 10 on the *Billboard* chart. The success even rubbed off at home, where the album crept to number 6 in March.

It was during this period that Led Zeppelin built its notorious reputation for being other than human through debauchery on the road. From their first visit to the States, where an amazed 19-year-old Robert Plant was agog at the fact that he could walk down Los Angeles's Sunset Strip shirtless, blond locks flowing behind him as girls fought for his attention, the band member's heads were turned by the physical pleasures that fame could bring them—and let them get away with. Jimmy Page had been through this mill once already with the Yardbirds, but it was nothing compared to the bacchanalian levels his new group would scale. From the beginning, Cole led his young charges into battle with adoring groupies and irate hotel managers.

Most notorious amongst the legion tales is the red snapper incident, in which a fish caught directly from the window of Cole's Seattle hotel room was "introduced" to a naked red-head groupie who was tied to the bed. As the drunken entourage, including a very refreshed John Bonham, encouraged him, Cole poked the nose of the fish into the girl's vagina with the charming enquiry, "How does your red snapper like this red snapper?" Cole remains unrepentant about his behavior then as on previous and subsequent occasions, claiming he was merely educating his young charges in the ways of the road. As he told Stephen Davis, author of *Hammer of the Gods*, "Robert and Bonzo didn't know anything, they were kids. It was the second tour that was the one. We were hot and on the way up and no one was watching too closely. You could fucking play." Whether it was wheeling Jimmy Page on a room service trolley into a hotel suite full of young girls or organizing motorbike races down corridors of hotels, the largely amoral Cole did whatever it took to relieve the boredom that set in during the constant touring.

In a recent interview in Q magazine, however, Plant distanced himself from many of the incidents claimed by Cole. He claimed the band responsible for the red snapper episode was actually the New York psychedelic act Vanilla Fudge, which was then a support act for Led Zeppelin, although Plant admits that members of his band and their wives were present for much of the freak show.

In particular, Plant dismisses much of Richard Cole's book, *Stairway to Heaven*. "Richard was not a happy camper and had a few drug problems when he was with Zeppelin," Plant told Q, "so he started subsidizing his habit by telling those stories. He was amalgamating and condensing all the stuff with all the bands he'd worked with and putting them all down to Led Zeppelin, because he knew our name would sell 'em rather than Vanilla Fudge or—God help 'em—Herman's Hermits."

The tale entered the Led Zeppelin lexicon, however, and along the way the fish morphed into a shark, possibly helped along the way by the Frank Zappa song "The Mud Shark" (from 1971's *Fillmore East* album), in which he relates the tale, complete with mud shark, and attributes the incident to Vanilla Fudge. As the legend of the fish grew, so did its association with Led Zeppelin, and people eventually, wrongly, came to the consensus that it was Led Zeppelin in a motel room with a shark.

The etymology of these tales aside, the effect of the carnage—real or invented—was a burgeoning myth around the band: they were the most outrageous and dangerous boys you could possibly know. The more their myth grew, the more they were encouraged to wilder excesses. While Cole led them on, Peter Grant watched their back with a wad of cash to silence anyone who complained. They were on their way to being the biggest band in the world and they were untouchable, so what was a poor lonely boy, thousands of miles from his provincial English home, to do?

Add this reputation for extravagance to the persistent, if ludicrous, rumor that three of the band members (Jones was the exception) had signed over their souls to the Devil in exchange for this lifestyle and success, and you have a stew that proved irresistible to a generation of kids loaded up on booze and bongs.

Amid the chaos on the road, the band recorded a follow-up album. Ducking into studios between gigs throughout 1969, they recorded riffs and songs and lyrics they had written in hotels, had left over from the first album, or made up on the spot. Plant was gaining confidence as a lyric writer, and stories of sexual exploits and groupies fill the songs, most obviously on "Living Loving Maid (She's Just a Woman)." It's the tale of an aging New York woman who annoyed the band by pushing younger girls out of the way at a studio to get to this hot new talent. Page humiliated her in front of the throng by making her sit outside in the corridor.

The end product was a rushing, 100-miles-an-hour album that seldom let up, and that reflected the group's hectic life. The pace had been pushed along by Atlantic, who, by the autumn of 1969, was harassing the band for a follow-up before the debut dropped out of the Top 20. Atlantic had wanted to release a second album by July, before the second U.S. tour, but the group stalled them and, thanks to Grant's outrageous contract demands, the label had to bite its lip. When they finally heard the album, the company couldn't have been happier, couldn't have been more *relieved*, that its most promising new group had traveled so far in a mere seven months.

Unlike the stylistically straightforward debut, *Led Zeppelin II* seemed to push boundaries few of the band's peers, with the possible exception of Jimi Hendrix, seemed to realize were there in the first place. "Whole Lotta Love," full of lust and delirious passion, Plant's orgasmic vocals entwined with Page's rampaging riff, rightly became a teenage anthem. Such is the timeless power of the song that it is still the theme music to Britain's longest-running and highest-rated TV music show, *Top of the Pops*. Elsewhere on the album, the hard-driving riffage of "Ramble On," "Heartbreaker," and "Living Loving Maid" are leavened by the lightness of touch on "Thank You" and the smoldering cod-Delta blues of "Bring It On Home." Even the faintly ludicrous "Lemon Song" is a harbinger of things to come: it's the first real outing of what Page wanted most from his then-undiscovered vocalist while still dreaming about Led Zeppelin two years earlier—a sparring partner for his guitar. But mostly, *Led Zeppelin II* was the blueprint for the explosive changes of tempo and volume that would come to a head on the band's fourth album.

Led Zeppelin II entered a market already in thrall to the Beatles' swan song *Abbey Road*, the Rolling Stones' *Let It Bleed*, and the close folk harmonies of Crosby, Stills & Nash. In the first week of release in the United States, *Led Zeppelin II* hit the charts with a thud at number 199, but a week later made one of the largest leaps in the history of the *Billboard* chart, up to number 15. Climbing to number 2, it was fended off by *Abbey Road* until Christmas week, when it finally toppled the Fabs from the number 1 spot. The album stayed at number 1 for another two months, finally surrendering only to Simon & Garfunkel's classic *Bridge Over Troubled Water*.

Led Zeppelin was now a bona fide superstar band. In the space of a single year it had become one of the highest-selling acts in the world, clocking up $5 million in album sales in the United States alone.

After four mammoth U.S. tours, a European trek that boasted 21 two-hour shows in a single month, two albums, and the stress of trying to be accepted in their own country, all within 15 months, the members of Led Zeppelin were exhausted. Page was stick-thin and ill again. Plant was frazzled by the constant change of pace that touring engenders, so nervously exhausted by his rapid rise from anonymous hippie weirdo to marauding rock god that he was wracked with self-doubt and the fear that he was unable to live up to fans' expectations. Plant had always felt his role in the group was undervalued both by critics and even his fellow band members, and he felt his talents were seen as inferior to the musicianship and songwriting skills of Page and Jones. Grant constantly had to reassure his singer that all that mattered was what the kids thought—and even Plant could see, from their broiling, reeling reactions at concerts, that the fans adored him.

Apart from the fans, however, the majority of Americans were incredibly conservative, their sense of security in such turbulent times threatened even further by the mere sight of hippies walking down the street and the changing values they represented. The white population particularly was having its way of life stripped away, the values they had held dear for decades eroded by civil rights and a tidal wave of social freedoms that its younger generation was both demanding and getting. For every kid that was turned on at Led Zeppelin's gigs, there were a hundred "straights" ready to spit at them in the street for their long hair and "faggot" clothing. Guns were pulled on them, cops wanted to bust them, death threats were common, restaurants wouldn't serve them, and hotels requested they not use the pool for fear of the band infecting other guests (with what, exactly, no one really knew).

On one particularly instructive occasion at the airport in Raleigh, North Carolina, two drunk sailors were goading Plant and Page about the length of their hair. The situation was resolved when Peter Grant lifted the two sailors off their feet, one in each hand, and roared, "What's your fucking problem, Popeye?"

As the 1960s drew to a close, a change of direction was in the air both for the counterculture and for Led Zeppelin. After the helter-skelter pace of the previous decade, a decade which had seen more social changes than any other 10-year period in peacetime history, reflection was needed. The peace and quiet required would be reflected in Led Zeppelin's new batch of songs.

At Plant's suggestion, he and his wife Maureen, Jimmy and his girlfriend Charlotte, a couple of roadies, and Plant's dog Strider decamped to a remote cottage with no electricity, called Bron-Y-Aur (the name means "golden breast"), in Wales. Plant remembered the cottage from a childhood family holiday. It was the very antithesis of the life they had led for the past 18 months. Although it was never meant to be a working holiday, inevitably the guitars came out at night as everyone sat around the fire hearth, plunging hot pokers into their cider and smoking Moroccan hash by the brick-load. The bulk of these songs would appear on the band's third album, but other snatches were kept back and would gradually surface throughout Led Zeppelin's career.

Led Zeppelin III, spawned in the quietude of the Welsh hills and released in October 1970, is very special indeed. Recorded partly back in London and, significantly, partly at Headley Grange, the country manor house where they would later record the fourth album, it has been undervalued for years and is only now experiencing something of a revival amongst a newer generation of fans not weighed down by preconceptions. Although it had the poorest chart perform-ance of all Led Zeppelin albums, *Led Zeppelin III* is perhaps the most cohesive set the band ever recorded, and it was the result of the first intensive songwriting burst between Page and Plant as equal partners. To dismiss it as their "acoustic album," as so many have done in the past, is reductive and lazy. Nobody of sound mind could call "Immigrant Song," "Celebration Day," or "Since I've Been Loving You" anything other than full-blown electric rockers. Even "Gallows Pole," a traditional English folk song, is driven by Bonham's relentless drumming and an underlying fuzzed-up guitar.

The main by-product of the Bron-Y-Aur songs' acoustic genesis was a newfound groove. Also significant is the lyrical development of Plant, who found confidence in writing about both personal experiences and his fascination with Celtic mythology while finally being able to incorporate his love of West Coast American bands. All these things would come to a head on their next album.

Yet again, the press slammed the group, many criticizing them for abandoning their rock roots. These were often the very same people who had disliked the first two albums for being all blues bluster with no substance. Whatever the critics stated at the time, however, there is no denying both the quality of the songs on *Led Zeppelin III* and the fact that, as evidenced on the album, this was a band that was stretching itself beyond recognition, finding layers of subtlety that even they had only before glimpsed in themselves.

Work on the album had continued throughout the summer, along with yet another American tour, during which they were demanding—and getting—a minimum fee of $25,000 per show, far more than most other bands could even dream of. The tour finished at New York's Madison Square Garden; their fee for the gig was $100,000. When *Led Zeppelin III* was finally released, it held the number 1 spot on the U.S. charts for a month. Even so, it has the distinction of being their lowest-selling studio album: like their 1976 release *Presence*, it sold a mere six million copies.

The beating that Led Zeppelin took from the press and the fact that during interviews they were finally reduced to dispiritedly bemoaning how they were still misunderstood led to rumors that a split was imminent. Although the rumors were dismissed by Plant with a single word—"crap"—they persisted, especially as the group seemed to all but disappear for the next few months. But expectations for the band became even greater. Would they ever resurface? Could they again come back and stretch themselves even further creatively?

The answer would be their trump card, a song they had been working on slowly over the previous six months that was going to blow everything done before out of the air. No one knew just how much "Stairway to Heaven" was going to change rock music.

boogie with Stu: recording Led Zeppelin IV

In early 1971 there was one major question the music press couldn't answer for their readers: Where was Led Zeppelin? The media, largely denied access to the band due to their own short-sightedness, couldn't ignore the group even if they didn't particularly hold much truck with their music. The kids wanted Led Zeppelin even if the music critics didn't, and therefore they were forced to cover the band. But where the hell were they? They hadn't been seen since September 1970, not even to tour after the release of their last album. Was it over? Had the flame that burned so brightly over the previous two years simply extinguished itself?

The answer, in short, was no, although the press was all too eager to report otherwise. In the U.K., *Melody Maker* and *New Musical Express* were running stories of an impending split almost weekly. Peter Grant would neither confirm nor deny the rumors, adding to the mystery already surrounding the band. To be fair to the press, however, Led Zeppelin, though on a creative high, was at a low point. Stung by the critics' reaction to *Led Zeppelin III* and shaken by its comparatively poor sales (only a month at number 1? How shocking!), the band simply decided to retreat. Peter Grant took his incessantly touring act off the road for only the second time in two years to give them space to regroup their thoughts. Those two years had seen them go from zero to 160 miles-per-hour in no time at all, and their nerves were tighter than fencing wire, their physical health ravaged.

There was also the internal pressure of needing to keep ahead of the pack. Having three platinum albums meant that Led Zeppelin could stake a reasonable claim to being the biggest band on the planet, even though no one outside their fan base knew it. The Rolling Stones garnered many more headlines, but then again, they were much more accessible to the press. Mick Jagger in particular courted the very publicity that Led Zeppelin shunned. Altamont, drug busts, and the end of Jagger's very public affair with Marianne Faithfull were perfect tabloid newspaper material. Those same papers were largely unaware that Led Zeppelin existed, yet Page, Plant, Bonham, and Jones were selling out bigger shows and shifting more albums. And the audience for each act was different. While the Stones continued to attract new young fans, their audience was still mostly the same one they had built up throughout the 1960s, a fan group now in its late 20s and early 30s. Led Zeppelin, however, was attracting a whole new following of teenaged kids and young adults in their early 20s. It was an age gap of only a couple of years, but this was the *Clockwork Orange* generation, rock fans to whom the Rolling Stones represented the passing decade, while their heroes, Led Zeppelin, were all about now and the future.

Over the previous two years, particularly after their first night playing in San Francisco as support to Country Joe & the Fish, the band was on a rock pilgrimage, which they pursued with missionary zeal. At that particular Fillmore

West show, Peter Grant had told them that they had to win over San Francisco to have any chance in the States. Led Zeppelin came out firing. They had been billed merely as a supporting act, stepping in at the last moment after the Jeff Beck Group had pulled out, but they felt they had to blow everyone else off the stage. They knew they could do it, so they did, and little dented their self-belief in their ability ever again. "It felt like a vacuum," Page told writer Cameron Crowe. "First this row, then that row—it was like a tornado and it went rolling across the country."

So now that they had time to take stock, the next question was, "Where do we go from here?" Some years after *Led Zeppelin IV*'s release, Page acknowledged to biographer Ritchie Yorke the pressure felt within the band. "We felt not only that the new album would make or break us but that we had to prove something to ourselves." Led Zeppelin was desperate to be taken seriously by the critics. The band craved affirmation that their songs were heavyweight, not just heavy—that they were worthy of their exalted status and not just a hype, as so many still wanted to believe.

In late 1970 Plant and Page returned to Bron-Y-Aur to start work in earnest on songs for the fourth album. The importance of the tiny cottage cannot be overstated. Its ambience and setting were so special to Page and Plant that it even received a special mention on the sleeve of *Led Zeppelin III*, credited as "painting a somewhat forgotten picture of true completeness." The same credit for the cottage also appears on *Physical Graffiti*, and then again on the Page and Plant reunion album *No Quarter*. (Plant ultimately bought the cottage.) As on their previous spring visit, they were again holed up without electricity. This time, however, it was the middle of winter. Regardless of the cold, they once more had the space to develop ideas that had only been sketches on the road, or that had surfaced during their previous sojourn but been put aside.

In December, the band moved into Island Studios in Basing Street, London (later bought by producer Trevor Horn and now operating as SARM West studios) to record the basic tracks for *Led Zeppelin IV*. Most of their previous recorded work had been completed in similar studios, but after the bucolic idyll of Bron-Y-Aur, it didn't feel right. These songs had been constructed much more organically, influenced by their rural surroundings and slowly developed and crafted. With their previous albums, Led Zeppelin had to rush everything, fitting songwriting between and around their heavy touring commitments and recording snatches of songs in studios all over the United States and United Kingdom, splicing the various tapes together later. Now, finally, Grant had given them some time to sit still and concentrate on the songs without being held to ransom by time.

The studio's latest technology wasn't bringing out the best in either the band or their new songs. Page explained his attitude toward studios in general to Yorke: "I get terrible studio nerves. Even when I've worked out the whole thing beforehand at home. I get terribly nervous playing anyway, particularly when I've worked out something that turns out to be a little above my normal capabilities. When it comes to playing in the studio, my bottle goes. I might as well be back years ago making all those dreadful studio records." This from the top dog session guitarist of the 1960s.

With the Christmas holidays approaching, the band took a break and went home to be with their families and to think. According to engineer Andy Johns, who had also worked on the band's previous two albums, Led Zeppelin regrouped after Christmas at Stargroves, Mick Jagger's house. Johns had recently finished working on the Rolling Stones' *Sticky Fingers* album, which had been recorded on the band's mobile studio (later to be made famous in the Deep Purple song "Smoke on the Water"). Johns says he suggested to Page that Led Zeppelin return to a similar approach, as they had done with some of the third album. If indeed they did start out at Stargroves—and Johns is the only person to have ever mentioned it—the stay was very short-lived. Johns claims the main reason they left was that Jagger wanted too much money for renting his house and Page was unwilling to pay, although they would later use the estate to record their album *Houses of the Holy*.

"You really do need the sort of facilities where you can take a break for a cup of tea and a wander around the garden," Page told Yorke. "Instead of that feeling of walking into a studio, down a flight of steps and into fluorescent lights. To work like that you've got to program yourself, telling yourself that you're going to play the solo of your life."

The obvious location was Headley Grange, a manor house in Hampshire that had served the band as a rehearsal space and had been used to record parts of their previous album. Headley Grange was built as a "poorhouse" in 1795. Such buildings were common in the United Kingdom, particularly throughout the Victorian era, providing food and accommodation for the most destitute people in return for work. As their very name suggests, poorhouses were grim dwellings. In November 1830, Headley Grange was the scene of a riot as residents protested against their treatment and conditions. In 1870 it was converted into a private dwelling and remained as such for the next 100 years. By the time Led Zeppelin moved in it was in poor repair and still without central heating. The members of the band and entourage appreciated the manor house for many reasons, but comfort was not one of them.

"Headley Grange was horrible," according to John Paul Jones. "It was cold and damp. I remember we all literally ran in when we arrived, in a mad scramble to get the driest rooms. There was virtually no furniture, no pool table, no pub nearby. It was so dull that it really focused your mind on getting the work done."

"The main reason they used Headley Grange was that it was cheap," Richard Cole has less reverently claimed. "The old woman who owned it couldn't believe her luck when we said we wanted to rent her crumbling old ruin in the middle of winter. The only one who actually liked being there was Jimmy. I think he enjoyed the fact that it was haunted, and he got himself a little room up at the very top of the house on the third floor, and he'd be there with his little electric fire."

The laid-back, rural atmosphere suited the newly rich band in several ways. Away from tours and cities, they could pretend to be country squires, something that appealed to the rebellious nature of those knocking down the deep-seated class divisions so valued by many Brits. Money and gentrification was for the aristocracy and whoever else was privileged enough to be invited into such circles.

Traditionally, those who had worked their way up the class ladder came from industry or commerce, but now there was a new breed of nouveau riche: the rock star. When the money came flooding in it was amusing to these musicians—who had been labeled as "outsiders" and "outlaws"—to act the part of the landed gent, corrupting the essence of "class" and effectively giving the finger to the very establishment who would rather that these hairy oiks stayed where they belonged. Obvious trappings of wealth and "breeding," such as Rolls Royces and country estates, were bought as quickly as possible by rock stars ever since the Beatles were numbered among the wealthiest people in the land. It was a poke in the eye of society's controlling hierarchy by the new super-rich, and they were determined to have as much fun with it as possible.

Austere as Headley Grange might have been, the band was hardly living like monks. According to Cole, they and their attendants "ate like million-dollar boy scouts" while consuming lakes of alcohol. "There weren't any serious drugs around the band at that point, just dope and a bit of coke," Cole recalled. "Mostly, we had an account at a shop in the village, and we'd go down there regularly and collect huge quantities of cider." When not rehearsing or recording, the band could go shooting (a terrifying prospect, considering their recreational intake at the time), walk through the local countryside, fish, or, in the case of John Bonham, wander down to the nearest pub dressed in a tweed jacket and cap, the day-to-day uniform of a country squire. "They found an old shotgun at the house and would go out hunting squirrels," Cole said. "Not that they ever hit anything."

A week of rehearsals was the immediate business of the day. According to John Paul Jones, only "Stairway to Heaven" and "The Battle of Evermore" were brought along by Plant and Page in anything approaching an advanced state. The rest of the tracks that were eventually included on the album were written almost entirely at Headley Grange. Even so, the band did have around a dozen demo'd and partially recorded pieces of songs, mostly from Bron-Y-Aur during the sessions for *Led Zeppelin III*, or from the week at Island Studios.

In fact, they had enough song snippets to mull over the idea of releasing a double album. According to Plant, the band only rejected the idea as late as February: "We decided not this time, but we've been saying not his time since the second album." As it turned out, it wasn't until their sixth studio album, *Physical Graffiti*, that they finally stretched to four sides.

The studio truck arrived a week into the sessions. Finally, recording could begin in earnest. And when the songs went onto tape, they flowed incredibly quickly. Part of the reason was certainly the location: the band was relaxed around the Grange, and with the studio parked outside, they could record at any time of the day or night, getting instant takes. Said Page, "In a way it was a good method. The only thing wrong was that we'd get so excited about an idea that we'd really rush to finish its format to get it on tape."

Black Dog

Astonishingly, apart from a few retakes and the odd solo, after a week of rehearsals Led Zeppelin spent only a further six days recording the album at Headley Grange.

One of the first orders of business was to run through any songs that anyone, particularly John Paul Jones, wanted to put on the table. Although the Plant-and-Page partnership was responsible for the majority of Led Zeppelin's output, Page claims that Jones was always encouraged to initiate song-writing as well. "Black Dog" was a riff that Jones brought along to the sessions, and the band immediately wanted it to be as heavy as possible, allowing them to open Led Zeppelin IV with a thundering track, just as they had on the previous two albums with "Whole Lotta Love" and "Immigrant Song" respectively.

Going through the album with Ritchie Yorke just after it had been finished, Plant said of "Black Dog": "The band is really getting attuned to time skips. We were messing around when the other lads suddenly come up with that passage on "Black Dog." They just played it, fell about all over the floor for 10 minutes in fits of laughter, played it again, burst into more laughter, then put it down on tape." Judging by this behavior, it's probably fair to say that large quantities of hash were also playing a role in the writing process.

The density and weight of the song was the result of four different Jimmy Page guitar parts tracked together through two compressors and distorted through the mic amp, a combination worked out by Andy Johns after he was given carte blanche by Page to experiment. One of the song's most unusual structures is the vocals leading into the breaks, a trick Page admits they lifted from Fleetwood Mac's "Oh Well" from the 1969 Play On album. Describing the arrangement of the song as "a bit of a hairy one," Page gives the credit to Jones for not only the initial riff but also working out the difficult timings. Jones, in turn, claims that Bonham worked out the seemingly impossible turnaround. "We struggled with it," Jones admitted, "until Bonzo figured out that you could just count four-time through it as if there was no turnaround."

The song became an instant crowd favorite, and it is probably the track that Led Zeppelin played live the most throughout its career. Seldom dropped from their set, it would eventually replace "Whole Lotta Love" as their encore. The song that had formerly defined them would be reduced to a couple of bars before blasting into "Black Dog."

The song's title came from an old black Labrador that hung around the Grange. Nobody knew who owned it, but it would disappear at night and come in and sleep all day, something Plant recalls as being a "powerful image at the time." Again, some fine Moroccan herb may well have enhanced the picture.

Rock and Roll

"Rock and Roll" was "found" when Bonham started playing the drum pattern from "Keep a' Knockin'" by Little Richard. Having difficulty with "Four Sticks," Bonham started bashing out the beat in frustration, and Page just joined in on guitar. The location was an essential part of the process.

"We had drums in the hall and sometimes in the room with us as well, and the amplifiers were all over," Page told author and Led Zeppelin chronicler Robert Godwin. "When Bonzo was in the hall Jones and I were out there, with earphones, with the two sets of amps in the other rooms and cupboards and things. A very odd way of recording, but when you've got the whole live creative process going on that's how things like 'Rock and Roll' come out."

The initial burst of the song only lasted about 15 seconds before coming to a halt, but when the band listened back to the tape it was obvious that there was already a song there. As it progressed, Plant improvised lyrics and Ian Stewart, the man who ran the mobile studio (but who was better known as the Rolling Stones' piano player and who is recognized as one of the great boogie woogie pianists of all time), came in from the truck to add the rollicking keyboard part. The whole song, according to Page, was worked out and recorded in about 15 minutes, and only three takes.

Interestingly, Robert Godwin advances the theory that Fleetwood Mac also had a hand in influencing "Rock and Roll." At the time, Peter Green was still Fleetwood Mac's driving musical force and the band was a respected blues act, very different from the soft-rock, Stevie Nicks–fronted version of the late 1970s. Fleetwood Mac did spend some time living in Headley village, although it's unclear whether or not this was while Led Zeppelin was recording at the Grange. In their 1970 live set, Fleetwood Mac included a version of "Keep a' Knockin'," a number that bears a strong resemblance to "Rock and Roll." As Godwin points out in his CD companion book on the making of *Led Zeppelin IV*, it's unlikely that a remake of "Keep a Knockin'" and the use of the vocal idea from "Oh Well" for "Black Dog" would have come about if Fleetwood Mac hadn't been strongly influential at the time.

The Battle of Evermore

"The Battle of Evermore," largely written at Bron-Y-Aur, is Led Zeppelin's most English of folk songs. It clicked into place when Page picked up a mandolin that Jones had brought along to the Grange. Although he had never really played the instrument before, Page started picking out some chords and the song simply coalesced around them. Page now jokingly dismisses his first attempts at the instrument, saying the melody was more governed by his limitations than his abilities: "I suppose all mandolin players would have a great laugh 'cos it must be the standard thing to play those chords, but possibly not with that approach."

The lyric is most obviously influenced by J.R.R. Tolkien's classic trilogy of books, *The Lord of the Rings*. There are references throughout the song to "the Dark Lord" and ringwraiths, and the opening words even refer to the "Queen of Light." In Tolkien's story, the Dark Lord Sauron searches for a ring of power that will give him absolute dominance over the known world. His special envoys on his search are nine "undead" men, the ringwraiths (or Nazgûl). The Queen of Light is the elf Galadriel, who offers sanctuary and counsel to the band of warriors and hobbits who have agreed to destroy the ring sought by Sauron. The song's lyric combines these references with others that were influenced by Plant's reading matter of the time, about the border wars that England waged with its Celtic neighbors during the Middle Ages.

Even by the "folksy" standards of its third album, this was a radical departure for Led Zeppelin. Plant described the lyric as more of a playlet than a song, and said that, after writing it, he realized that he needed another voice on the track. Fairport Convention had always been a group favorite (remember, Led Zeppelin had been toying with the idea of becoming an English folk act before Page saw Bonham play), and so their troubled ex-singer Sandy Denny was invited to sing alongside Plant on the track when the band moved back to Island Studios from Headley Grange. Denny had recently left Fairport Convention after performing on three of the band's landmark albums, including the classic 1969 *Unhalfbricking*. Although she was without doubt the pre-eminent female English folk voice of her generation, most people outside the world of folk know her mainly through her work on "The Battle of Evermore." A notoriously heavy drinker, she died in April 1978 from injuries sustained when she drunkenly fell down some stairs.

Stairway to Heaven

And then there was "Stairway to Heaven." Page had worked hard on the song over the previous seven months, particularly while at the Bron-Y-Aur cottage. In interviews, the band had alluded to the track, but nothing concrete was known about it. Page told one London music journalist, "It's an idea for a really long track. You know how 'Dazed and Confused' is broken into sections? Well, we want to try something new with the organ and acoustic parts building up and building up and then the electric part might start. It could be a 15-minute track."

The kernel of the song had come about during Page's and Plant's first visit to Bron-Y-Aur. The guitarist subsequently spent time working out the six- and twelve-string parts and how to shift between the song's various gears. After returning from the cottage, Page recorded basic demos of the component parts at his eight-track-equipped home studio, which housed the mixing desk that the Who had used to record their landmark *Live at Leeds* album the year before. These tapes were strictly works in progress for Page to play to the band, to give them an idea of what he was striving for, but they have surfaced on bootleg albums over the years.

The idea was to record a track that encompassed everything the group had striven toward over the previous two years, building gradually until it exploded in a huge crescendo. Andy Johns was with the program very early. "I remember saying to Jimmy that I wanted to work on a song that started off real quiet and got bigger and bigger," the engineer said, "and Pagey said, 'Oh, don't worry, I've got one of those for this album.'"

Another initial spur for the song came from Beatle George Harrison. He met Bonham one night and told the drummer that the problem with Led Zeppelin was they didn't do any ballads. Bonham relayed the comment to the rest of the band and, as a nod to Harrison, Page included the first few notes of the Beatles' "Something" when writing the "Stairway to Heaven" tune.

Having written a number of short sections and put them all down on tape, it was now a matter of Page slotting them together until they worked in sequence, constantly referring back when he felt there was something else he could add in or a section that would bind two others. The structure was finally worked out. When it came to playing the final version, events again progressed quickly.

The first evening after the mobile studio arrived, Page and Jones sat down and wrote out the sheet music for the finished, stitched-together version of the song. Plant and Bonham went to the pub. The next day the band ran through the entire song for the first time, with tapes rolling. They immediately knew they had something special, something that brought together everything they had glimpsed as being possible at that very first rehearsal. Even so, it took a few beginning-to-end run-throughs to get anywhere near the final version. Bonham in particular was having trouble getting the timing for the 12-string fanfare into the guitar solo.

A bootleg recording of the session reveals how the song was built up. The first version is an acoustic instrumental, with Page laying out the whole song for the rest of the band and repeatedly returning to the opening chord pattern. Interestingly, Jones has already worked out a spidery organ accompaniment, so the pair must have rehearsed extensively the night before while Plant and Bonham were in the pub.

The second take began at the point most listeners would now recognize as the middle of the final version, with Page and Jones attempting to find a way from the bridge into the final guitar solo. The next run-through was similar, but managed to get through the section and into the solo before Page went off on a tangent that eventually led nowhere and was soon abandoned. On the fourth take, the band reached the end for the first time. Finally, on the fifth take, they were ready to attempt a complete run-through with guide vocals.

Sitting listening to the others gradually massage the sections into shape, Plant grabbed his notebook and started writing out lyrics. An amazed Page later claimed that Plant wrote the majority of the lyric there and then. "There's a first rehearsal tape of the song and 60 per cent of the lyrics Robert came up with on the spot." Plant has called the track "unnaturally easy" to record, saying he felt as if something had been pushing him when he was writing the lyrics. "There was something saying, 'You guys are OK, but if you want to do something timeless, here's a wedding song for you.'" Whether this was said with a straight face or not, it all adds to the myth.

The first complete run-through, however, has only two verses, and most of this lyric was changed by the time the band came to the final version. The lyric changed, in fact, throughout the various recorded versions, and was finalized throughout the following week or so before the band headed for Island Studios.

Remarkably, the sixth take of the song is a near-finished version, the lyric already closer to the final product. They are far from complete, however, as is demonstrated by the line, "If the stores are all closed she can call in and see a movie," as well as by the absence of any mention of bustles or hedgerows. The drums were still some way off from being ready: Bonham continued to have trouble playing through the various sections, and in these takes he mostly settled for a few rimshots, which were gone by the final recording.

By the sixth take, Page's guitar solo at the end had already been largely written. The session tape finishes with Plant rhetorically asking Page, "That's all right, isn't it?" The guitarist, with no little understatement, replies, "Yeah, that's going to be very nice."

Although "Stairway to Heaven" was completely worked out at Headley Grange, the band decided to rerecord it when they got back to the Island Studios in London. Moving into Studio One, a massive room that was often used by orchestras, the group set up. Page sat in a tiny square of baffles that completely enclosed him and his acoustic guitar, while Jones sat by a Moog keyboard bass and Bonham sat at the back of the room. After one take, the band gathered in the control booth to listen to the playback. Almost everyone was amazed at what they were listening to. This was the track that would ensure that critics could no longer deny that Led Zeppelin was a real musical force. The one person who thought otherwise was Page.

Richard Digby-Smith, the young assistant studio engineer, remembered the session in some detail: "It was an amazing take," he recalled several years later. "Bonzo put down his sticks and put on his coat and said, 'That's that one nailed, then.' But Page wasn't happy and asked for another take. The rest, who were mildly incensed, reluctantly went back into the studio. Bonham grabbed his sticks, said, 'You always do this to us, Jimmy,' and stormed into the room and sat there with steam coming out of his ears. It was quite tense. They did another take and that was the one. Bonham just looked at Page and said something like, 'You bastard. You were right,' while Page just nodded and said, 'Yeah, that's what I wanted.'"

Next came Jones's accompaniment to the six-string guitar intro. Although there was speculation at the time that Jones was possibly playing a Mellotron or even a synthesizer, it is actually three different recorders—baritone, tenor, and soprano—that gives the intro its haunting, lilting quality.

All that remained now was the guitar solo. Warming up, Page ran through three different versions before the tapes were switched on. Wanting a different sound than that of his usual trademark Gibson, Page plugged in a Telecaster that Jeff Beck had given him. Digby-Smith again remembers the moment in detail: "I can still see Page playing the solo.

We did a lot of orchestral stuff in that room, and orchestral musicians don't like using headphones very much, so we had these big Tannoy monitors, which we would wheel in for the playbacks and bolt to the floor. So Page used these things for the solos.

"There were these four big orange speakers with Page standing between them, and we played him back through them as loud as possible, and he just leaned up against the speakers with a cigarette hanging out of his mouth and rattled out that solo." So much for Page's studio nerves.

Speaking about the song 20 years later for a BBC radio documentary, Page admitted that the concept of the song was difficult to get across to the rest of the band.

"The whole idea was to have this huge crescendo," he said, "starting with something that was very intimate and bringing the power of Bonzo's drums in at a later point, so it gave it that extra kick. Now that everyone's so familiar with it, this may not make a lot of sense, but it was quite a complicated song to get across to everybody."

But they did get it, and even Page the perfectionist seemed pleased with the end result. "Everything can be better in hindsight," he told the BBC, "but at the time I was pretty happy with what we'd done because it had such a great atmosphere. I had to have a few attempts at mixing it, mind you, and I must admit, that took longer than the actual recording."

Misty Mountain Hop

According to Plant, "Misty Mountain Hop," the song that opens the second side of the original vinyl album, is "a song for anyone who ever got waylaid when they were going somewhere". More specifically, it's about a bunch of hippies getting busted for possession of marijuana in a park.

Two suggestions about its lyrical genesis have been made: that it was a scene that Plant came across while walking in San Francisco; and that it was about a love-in in Hyde Park, London, that was broken up by the police. Regardless of the song's inspiration, it also contains references to Tolkien's *The Lord of the Rings*. The Misty Mountains, which are also featured in *The Hobbit*, are above the Mines of Moria, through which the Fellowship of the Ring have to travel and where the wizard Gandalf battles the mighty Balrog. With Led Zeppelin, the Misty Mountains represent a better place "where spirits fly," and people are free of society's constraints.

"Misty Mountain Hop" was written entirely at Headley Grange, the basic riff being found by John Paul Jones early one morning while sitting at the piano after he had risen earlier than the others.

Four Sticks

Although "Four Sticks" was also written entirely at Headley, it wasn't until the group returned to Island Studios that the final recording was made. Jones had left the other members to their work for a couple of days because of an unspecified illness. By the time he returned, Page had come up with the basic rhythms and tune for "Four Sticks." "I had real problems working out where the beat should go," Jones said, "because rhythmically it was quite unusual, but I was the only one in the band who could do that because of my background as an arranger." Even so, Bonham couldn't work out the rolling drum pattern, and the song was temporarily abandoned when work began on "Rock and Roll."

Back at Island, they again tried to work out the rhythms, but Bonham still couldn't make it work. They even tried recording it with Page in front of the kit, playing drums along with Bonham. Frustrated, Bonham eventually put his drumsticks to one side and quaffed down a Double Diamond, a brand of British beer particularly popular in the 1970s. Suitably refreshed, he attacked his kit once more, this time picking up four drumsticks, two in each hand, held between thumb and forefinger and forefinger and middle finger.

"I couldn't get it to work," Page has since said, "and I still wouldn't know what it was if Bonzo hadn't done that. We would probably have kicked the track out." The final drum track was done in only two takes because Bonham was physically unable to do a third.

Page was also experimenting with different amps and mic placings to get the droning sound that comes into the middle of the song. The buzzing drone that arrives just toward the end was Jones playing a Moog synthesizer.

Going to California

If "The Battle of Evermore" is their most English folk song, "Going to California" is certainly Led Zeppelin's most American. In it are echoes of all those 1960s Californian groups in which Plant had been interested, and which Page had dismissed. Plant has described the song as being about the unrequited search for the "ultimate lady," and nobody sought for her more than the members of Led Zeppelin in their Californian playground of Los Angeles.

Although they had never mentioned it before, Page and Plant were besotted with Californian songstrel Joni Mitchell and, as ardent admirers of both her and her work, they wrote "Going to California" specifically as a tribute to the queen of the Hollywood canyons. "When you're in love with Joni Mitchell," Plant said in 1974, "you've really got to write about it now and again."

It's easy to see why Page and Plant were attracted to Mitchell, whose 1970 *Ladies of the Canyon* and the following year's *Blue* albums established her as one of the leading singer-songwriters of her day. Mitchell adapted her folk roots to include jazz, pop, avant-garde, and world music to create something unique, in much the same way that Led Zeppelin moved well beyond their blues influences. When Plant talked of being in love with Mitchell, however, he is more likely to have been talking in a musical, rather than a physical, sense.

The song initially came about during what Page describes as "another late night guitar twiddle" at Headley Grange, with the grounds of the house playing a part in the final recording. "We did 'Going to California' with all of us sitting outside on the grass playing mandolins and whatever else was around," Jones explained. "At one point you can actually hear an airplane going over, but we were always happy to leave that sort of thing in rather than lose a good take."

When the Levee Breaks

The final song on the album is arguably the second-most important track Led Zeppelin ever recorded, after "Stairway to Heaven." "When the Levee Breaks," which is based on a 1928 blues song by Memphis Minnie, was a track that they had tried to record before, but it never quite came out right. The problem was solved again by Bonham, again almost by accident, but it demonstrates more than any other track just how important Bonham was to Led Zeppelin's makeup. As Page has said, "Nobody other than John Bonham could have created that sex groove."

With all the instruments in the same room of the house, there was significant sound leakage between the amps, and Bonham couldn't get the clean yet massive sound he was hearing in his head reproduced on tape. According to Andy Johns, while the rest of the band was at the pub having a drink, he and Bonham set up a newly delivered kit out in the Grange's hallway, which doubled as the house's central stair-well, climbing three stories above their heads. Hanging two stereo mics above the kit, one about 10 feet from it, the other 20, Johns then ran the drums into two channels on the desk outside through an old echo unit. There was also, apparently, a mic on the kick drum, but it was never used; because of the balance of Bonham's brand new kit, the relative volume of the various components was already very good. Johns compressed the sound even further and was so startled by the results that he ran back into the house, shouting for Bonham to quickly come and listen. Hearing what had been captured on tape, Bonham exclaimed, "That's it! That's what I've been hearing!" At least, according to Johns.

Page, however, remembers it differently, and he also stakes a claim to "discovering" the sound. During his session days, the guitarist contends, he saw countless drummers bashing away at their kits in the studio, only to have them sound like biscuit tins in the mix, all because they were crammed into tiny isolation booths with microphones close to the drums. Page figured, rightly, that pulling the microphones away from the drums, or indeed the amps, would result in a much fuller ambience, one that would actually capture the true "live" sound of the instrument. Essentially, what you hear on "When the Levee Breaks" is not just the sound of Bonham's drumming, but the way in which the drums react to the acoustics of the room they were in. Although a slight echo was put onto the recording, what's on the album is pretty much what was played—one of the greatest drum sounds of all time, and the second-most sampled drum pattern in history (after Clyde Stubblefield's work on James Brown's "Funky Drummer").

Whichever way it happened, the song was sprung off the back of Bonham's drumming. According to Page, "We had been trying it before, but it was at the point Bonham's new kit appeared and was set up in the hall that the drum sound actually fired it along. You had this beautiful space and the sound was so phenomenal, that this was going to be the drum sound for "Levee." He had been saying all along, 'Wait until the drum kit arrives, everything's going to be fine!'"

But the drums weren't the only unusual effect used by Page and Johns on "When the Levee Breaks." In another master stroke, a backward echo was put on both Plant's harmonica and Page's guitar. A process that Page had come up with while still in the Yardbirds, it involved recording the instrument, then running the tape backward through an echo unit. Page is uncertain which Yardbirds song he first used the technique on, but he does admit that it was an adaptation of an earlier idea. "There had been backwards guitar before, but

I thought, 'Why not backwards echo?'" It all contributed to Page's master plan for the track, which he set out to make sound as ominous as possible. Even then it wasn't good enough for the pernickety producer, who today claims that the track only really sounds as it should on headphones.

And so, after just six days with the mobile studio, the band left Headley Grange and went back into Island Studios. There were still overdubs to record, plus Sandy Denny's vocal for "The Battle of Evermore." As it turned out, they would also rerecord "Four Sticks" and "Stairway to Heaven."

Their work rate is even more impressive when you factor in the three other songs they recorded that didn't make the album—"Boogie with Stu" (the Rolling Stones' Ian "Stu" Stewart), "Night Flight," and "Down by the Seaside"—versions of which turned up on *Physical Graffiti*.

From start to finish, from the trek to Bron-Y-Aur to Headley Grange and back to Island Studios, the whole venture took little more than two months, including the break over Christmas. It was so smooth and seamless a process that it appeared the band was blessed, that this album just couldn't put a foot out of place. That feeling would prove to be very premature, as Led Zeppelin was about to go through one of its few, uncharacteristic wobbles.

With the tracks completed at Island, all that remained was the mixing. Itching to get back on the road, however, the band put the album to one side for a short, scaled-down tour of British clubs, partly as a thank you to the promoters and fans who had first had faith in them, partly to test out the new songs on a live audience. With no album to promote, Plant would later describe the tour as pointless, but it did at least shut the papers up and quell rumors of the band splitting.

The tour ended in early April, and the group was desperate to get its new album out. In the original schedule, they were to mix the album in late February and release it in March, but the mixing still hadn't been addressed. The band members knew they had played out of their skins to record the best album of their career to date, and they were convinced that they were about to deliver something that would finally silence the dissenters. Reaction to the new material on the "Back to the Clubs" tour was also so strong that it was even more frustrating that they couldn't get the album out. Partially to assuage this frustration, partially to further dispel the rumors that they'd disbanded, Led Zeppelin played a BBC radio session, on John Peel's prosaically titled *Rock Hour*.

Of the three songs previewed at the session—"Black Dog," "Going to California," and "Stairway to Heaven"—only two made the final broadcast ("Black Dog," deemed at the time the least of the three, was dropped). The radio session has been endlessly bootlegged, and in 1997 it was released as part of the *BBC Sessions* album.

Andy Johns, meanwhile, convinced Page that the best studio for mixing the album in was Sunset Sound in Los Angeles, which he considered to have the truest sound available in the world. Willingly accepting the engineer's recommendation, Page flew with Johns to L.A. with the master tapes while the rest of the band stayed in Britain. And then all hell broke loose.

Johns's intentions proved to be not entirely honorable. Having recently recorded an album at Sunset Sound with a band that would later become the Knack, he was, in his own words, "seeing this chick" in L.A., and wished to rekindle the liaison. Between his last visit and February 1971, the studio monitors had been changed, and so they moved to a second studio in the complex, a mistake that Johns readily acknowledges. "We should have just gone home. But I didn't want to and I don't think Jimmy did, either. We only worked for about 10 days by the time we left and when we got back, the other guys wanted to hear the mixes, and so we went into Olympic Studios in London for a playback, which was another mistake. The only things that sound good in that room is stuff that has been recorded there."

Neither Johns nor Page had listened to the tapes at home since the mixing process and as the tracks rolled, so did eyes. The mix was awful, and sounded muddy and indistinct. The entire process had been a complete waste of time. Johns recalled that he and Page "crouched in the corner really embarrassed." The rest of the band was disgusted that so much time had already been wasted and that now the whole mixing process was to begin again. Only one track, "When the Levee Breaks," was salvaged from the original mix.

Returning to Island Studios with another engineer (Page claims that Johns just dropped out of view after the playback fiasco; Johns claims that, after that, "they just didn't need old Andy anymore, you know?"), the mixes were completed to everyone's satisfaction. The by-now-interminable process of getting the album on the streets was almost over.

Finally, in November 1971, *Led Zeppelin IV* was released, 13 months after the release of the band's previous album. Here was a group that had put out three classic albums within the space of 20 months, and now their fourth had taken just over a year. The reason for the final holdup? Arguments with Atlantic over the title and, more specifically, the cover, on which the band wanted to have no information. It was to be the biggest battle between the band and its label of Led Zeppelin's entire career, with neither side wanting to back down. But with Peter Grant going in to bat for the group, there was little chance of Led Zeppelin losing.

no quarter:
the cover art

One of the largest contributing factors to Led Zeppelin's ongoing mystique is the cover of *Led Zeppelin IV*. The lack of a title, the absence of any information, the tarot-derived illustration on the inner sleeve, and the use of mystical symbols to represent each member of the band all fueled the rumors that had circulated for years about Led Zeppelin's pact with the Devil and Jimmy Page's infatuation with arch-satanist Aleister Crowley. Wild theories about the dark meanings behind it all spread among fans like wildfire. Here, surely, was proof that their band, this group they cherished because of its very flirting with the dark side, was indeed locked into some dark Luciferian treaty.

Whether or not such an agreement was ever signed with Beelzebub—and let's face it, it's pretty unlikely—the reasons behind the cover and its symbols are probably far more bland than hormonal youth would like to believe. Even so, the art-work triggered one of the rare conflicts that Led Zeppelin had with its label.

Throughout their career Led Zeppelin's members had kept it simple, stripping every aspect of the band to its barest core. Their live shows relied almost solely on musicianship, old-fashioned stagecraft, and the quality of their songs for the power of their performance—there was none of the fancy lighting trickery of Pink Floyd or back-projected films and fire eaters of the Velvet Underground for Led Zeppelin. If they had a live gimmick, it was sheer, bludgeoning volume. It was a stripped-down philosophy that extended to their album sleeves and titles.

Self-titling the band's debut was not unique; calling the two that followed *Led Zeppelin II* and *Led Zeppelin III*, however, was pushing the concept. Such a move may have been awkward, but it was hardly without reason. Page was obsessed with letting the music do the talking, particularly after the debut's poor reviews and the constant accusations of hype and ripping-off that dogged his band. The music press, uninvited, put themselves between the band and its fans, telling the public that here was a group that was nothing but a corporate con, something being foisted upon them by the evil of "the Man." How else could the $200,000 advance paid out by Atlantic be explained away? The record company, heaven forbid, had obviously seen money in "them thar Led Zeppelin hills" when they should have been altruistically putting out the music for the sake of *art* and *the kids*. This was the Summer of Love, after all. Money-making was something to be despised, and anyone creaming profits off of "our" culture was to be suspected of nefarious intent.

It's a pattern that has held sway over music ever since hippies gained control of the musical moral high ground. As a musician, you were allowed to be rich as long as you didn't flaunt it in the faces of the fans, as long as you talked about not selling out and your desperate need to unload your tortured artistic soul. When punk exploded in the United Kingdom, the notion of "doing it for the kids" took hold of a whole new generation. Throughout the 1970s, rock stars had become ever more distant from their audience. From West

Coast acts such as the Eagles, or Crosby, Stills & Nash, locked away in their Laurel Canyon mansions, to Pink Floyd slowly building a wall of bricks between themselves and their audience during live performances, symbolizing the remote nature of the rock star, most major bands set themselves apart from their followers. It's one of rock's great paradoxes that the bigger you become and the more people you touch with your music, the further away from them you get. Plant even acknowledged this to Q magazine in a 2002 interview. "When you have an audience all over the world like Zeppelin did," the singer said, "back home you're not playing the Old Red Lion pub anymore. You become more remote from your audience and you're a generation removed from the average kid on the street. I understand why punk happened, why it had to happen. I still think the Damned singing, 'I got a new rose, I got a new rose' sounds fantastic."

Desperate to stay close to their idols, the indie kids who followed the original punks viewed selling out as the ultimate crime. It was all about being the downtrodden, grim-faced underclass who stoically held back the evil world of commerce through their musical badge of truth. The New Romantics flaunted their style rather than their wealth, but the indie bands of the mid-to-late-1980s, such as the Smiths, reveled in their proletarian grayness, and it wasn't until hip hop emerged that artists were again allowed crude displays of their money. But even then, that was permissible only if you were from the streets and were constantly reasserting your ghetto-fabulous credentials, as people such as Ice T so expertly managed throughout the 1990s, all the while living in the Hollywood Hills and amassing a fortune. Even now,

R & B stars are nothing if they're not flashing their Louis Vuitton leisure suits and diamond-studded teeth while "real" bands such as Travis, Green Day, or Limp Bizkit tread a thin line between being just like their fans and living a life few of the record buying public can afford.

None of this attitude is inherently bad, just hypocritical, and Led Zeppelin encountered a massive wall of it. Their biggest crime was not knowing how to deal with it, foolishly believing that people would eventually see beyond the surface and view them as they saw themselves. Their music was giving pleasure to millions, and they earned their stripes by touring constantly, wringing out their physical and nervous reserves for over two hours a night as they cavorted and contorted in front of their audience. But still the "hype" barbs were hurled at them, and when they got under the skin, they hurt.

So, how to reduce the risk of misunderstanding? Whereas most others would have mounted a charm offensive, for Page and the rest of the band, part of the answer was to give even less of themselves.

When the Beatles turned music upside down, they also turned the whole record industry inside out. Along with Bob Dylan, they were responsible for popular music being taken seriously as an art form and, as a consequence, they elevated album sleeve art to a similar status. Before the extremely ambitious and expensive cover for *Sgt. Pepper's Lonely Hearts Club Band*, sleeves had just been something for the record companies to wrap around the product, a basic and direct marketing tool. Yes, some labels had taken care over their sleeves, particularly the Blue Note jazz label, but even these had a graphic design integrity to them rather than an artistic worth. At best, early 1960s jackets were simplistic, often plugging the label's other artists on inner sleeves; at worst they were cheesy abominations bearing little relationship to what lay within. The record companies considered themselves to be the marketing experts, not the lowly musicians, and they thought it best that these lank-haired buffoons stay out of what they didn't know.

Because of this attitude, Led Zeppelin had been left unsatisfied with the covers of their first three albums. The black-and-white sleeve of the debut, picturing a Zeppelin airship bursting into flame at its mooring, did convey some of the explosive grace of Led Zeppelin's music, but it was also very downbeat and stark. The cover of *Led Zeppelin II*, which depicted the band as World War I pilots, was, in hindsight, a very campy image, while the sleeve for the third album was a disaster for the band. The cover was originally intended as a corruption of the rotating seasonal planting guides so beloved by gardening magazines, but the idea had been poorly communicated to the designer. When presented with the artwork, the band was disappointed that it looked cartoonish and childlike, more like a pop album, but, because of the speed at which Led Zeppelin recorded and released LPs, there was no time to change it fundamentally. The plan had been for the album's buyer to rotate the inner wheel, revealing through the diecut holes in the outer sleeve items that reflected the songs as it spun. Instead, it became a tacky compromise of abstract items and pictures of the group. With this new album, Led Zeppelin was determined to get it right.

Throughout the recording, discussions had continued within the band about what to call their new album. Everyone—the fans, the media—expected it to be called *Led Zeppelin IV*, and why not? Page's continued insistence that it was the music that spoke to their audience, and his desperation to avoid giving the press ammunition with which to shoot the group down, suggested that they would continue down this generic path. "It might be called *Led Zeppelin IV*," he said of the new album's title at the time. "Everybody expects that, but we might change it. We've got all sorts of mad ideas. I was thinking at one time of having four EPs, but frankly, the price of records now is extortionate and we want to keep the cost down."

Compared to such a bold concept, the format the band settled on was fairly straightforward. A single album in a gatefold sleeve was slightly extravagant, but hardly unusual at the time. At any rate, the problem that the record company had was not about what was on the sleeve: they were more concerned with what was left off.

Carrying his minimalist idea to its logical conclusion, Page decided he wanted no information on the sleeve at all, just an image. No band name, no album title, not even a corporate label logo. Nothing.

"It came to the point," the guitarist explained, "where we thought, Right, on the next album we'll make it untitled with no information whatsoever, virtually saying, 'If you don't like it, you don't have to buy it for the name'." It was actually quite a radical move. Even the nearest precedent, The Beatles' White Album, had the band's name embossed on the cover. But Peter Grant told the record company that Led Zeppelin didn't even want a catalogue number on the jacket.

"Names, titles, and things like that," Page told an interviewer when the album came out, "don't mean a thing. What does 'Led Zeppelin' mean? It doesn't mean a thing. What matters is our music. If we weren't playing good music, nobody would care what we called ourselves. If the music was good, we could call ourselves 'Cabbages' and still get across to our audience."

Plant was even more defiant. "With every cover we've had before," he told journalist Caroline Boucher, "what we've asked for hasn't been what we've got. We wanted a cover with no writing on it, not the Atlantic symbol or the 'up tight and outta sight' bit."

The record company was apoplectic. Here was their biggest act who, as far as the fans were concerned, had gone into hibernation over the winter, and now they wanted to come out with their new album, released a full year after the last one, carrying no identifying marks whatsoever. It was, according to one Atlantic executive, "commercial suicide." Beyond that lay an additional concern: if the company caved in and let the band do as they wished, what would their demands be next time? Would all their other acts take this as a precedent and start imposing all sorts of weird strictures?

The result was a standoff, with the band refusing to budge and the record company pleading with them that they were about to shoot themselves in the foot. Neither would give in, both believed they were totally in the right.

The tension within the band was building, too. Insiders have commented that it was the most internally fraught period the group had experienced. Negotiations moved at a snail's pace, further delaying the release of their masterwork. A European tour had been booked to coincide with the original release date, and now it looked like they would be on

Early days: (from left) Robert Plant, John Paul Jones, John Bonham, and Jimmy Page, 1970.

Left *Robert Plant in
"Golden God" mode
during the recording of*
Led Zeppelin IV.

Right *A fresh-faced
Jimmy Page in* 1967,
*during his tenure with
the Yardbirds—
a far cry from the
legendary wild man of*
Led Zeppelin tours.

The band give generously of themselves for a prerelease publicity session for Led Zeppelin IV, *1971.*

Above *On the "Back To The Clubs" tour, Southampton University, 1971. (Left: John Bonham in full "Bonzo" mode. Right: John Paul Jones, Robert Plant, and Jimmy Page.)*

Above *John Bonham never had much to do during acoustic sessions at Jimmy's house.*

Right *Bonzo in full "Rock and Roll" flight, 1973.*

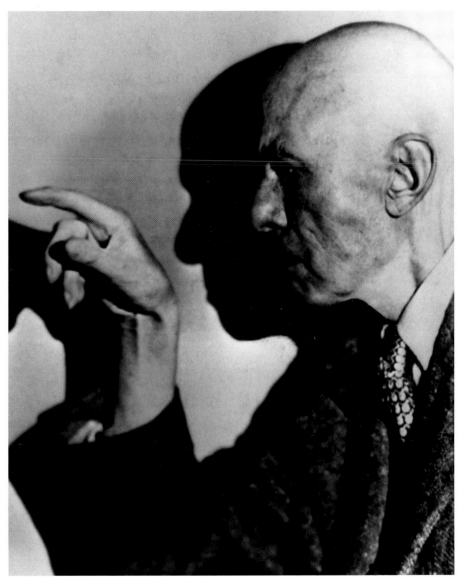

Aleister Crowley: The extent of the Great Beast's influence on the making of Led Zeppelin IV *is still hotly debated.*

Chateau Marmont: More publicity opportunities for the band: (from left) John Bonham, John Paul Jones, Robert Plant, and Jimmy Page.

The controversial symbols representing (from left) Page, Jones, Bonham, and Plant.

the road with nothing to promote. The March club tour had been one thing, but a full-scale European jaunt, followed by dates in the United States, was not to be wasted as a promotion opportunity. As it turned out, the tour would turn poisonous, but for another, far more sinister reason.

Arriving in Milan that July to headline at the 12,000-capacity Vigorelli Stadium, the band found that they were one of 28 acts playing that day. To keep control of the crowd, the authorities had flooded the stadium with fully-armed riot police, who were on tenterhooks. When Led Zeppelin finally took the stage the packed crowd, as was customary, went wild. The police panicked. The promoter asked the band to plead with the audience to stop lighting fires, cautioning that otherwise the police were going to wade in, but when a tear gas canister was fired at the stage, the band realized the "smoke" was not coming from fires, but from the police. Page called for the rest of the band to cut the performance short and do just one more song. As they launched straight into "Whole Lotta Love," tear gas stinging their eyes, the kids leapt back to their feet. The police charged them from the rear and, in a desperate attempt to get away, some of the audience climbed onto the stage.

By now the band could barely see each other, let alone the crowd, through the gas. Standing at the front of the stage, Richard Cole fought back the audience as the band ran off and the roadies tried to save the equipment. Cole yelled for everyone to leave the gear and run for it down a backstage tunnel. Losing their way in the mayhem, they barricaded themselves in the medical room while the riot raged above their heads. By the time they emerged, the stage and all their gear had been destroyed, and Bonham's roadie, Mick Hinton, had suffered a bad gash to his head and had to be carried on a stretcher to hospital. In the bar of their hotel later that evening, Bonham threatened to smash a bottle over the head of a journalist who was pestering the band, who were still badly shaken, for a quote.

Meanwhile, arguments with the record company persisted. Page was less than impressed with Atlantic: "They were all dead frightened of giving away too much. The album was a whole experiment, really, because everything was under-played, rightly or wrongly. Some people might consider that to be suicide. But it had to be done to satisfy our own minds after all the crap that had gone down in the newspapers."

Eventually the matter was settled for purely pragmatic reasons: the band refused to give the record company the master tapes unless it backed down. Faced with such staunch refusal by the band to compromise, the record company had little choice, especially when Grant rolled out the band's contract and again showed them the clauses relating specifically to artistic control. Atlantic was over a barrel.

Ironically, the very approach that the band took to pre-vent the sleeve from detracting from the music is the reason that the cover has come to have a strangely mysterious significance for the fans. The lack of any attempt to explain the images with a title has led people to assume that they have some greater significance, some deeper portent. On the face of it, the jacket for *Led Zeppelin IV* is reasonably straight-forward. It's not difficult to divine the symbolism of the image on the outer sleeve, but, as with all things Led Zeppelin, there are hidden depths and multiple layers of meaning.

The front cover shows a framed picture of an old man carrying a bundle of sticks on his back, slowly trudging back home after having collected his firewood. The picture is hung on the inside wall of an old cottage, the wallpaper peeling off the plaster. Open up the sleeve, and the back shows that the wall of the cottage has either been knocked down or fallen away. In the distance is a high-rise housing block, an estate the likes of which are found in every major city in the United Kingdom.

Built mainly in the late 1950s and early 1960s, tower blocks were supposed to be a utopian answer to the Victorian housing slums that had become decrepit and diseased. Many of them still had outside toilets and no heating. Architects convinced the local councils that the way to build for the future was up, not out. Thus the tower block was invented, a 20-story concrete abomination that was supposed to give everyone an equal opportunity to enjoy modern housing and conditions. The experiment quickly proved disastrous, as the maintenance on these buildings was huge and the councils couldn't afford their upkeep. Putting individuals into a utilitarian box only dehumanized them. As their inhabitants' respect for their surroundings quickly disappeared, the housing estates were vandalized and covered in graffiti. Elevators stopped working, plumbing broke down, and the cheap materials used in construction started to crumble. The tower blocks quickly became worse slums than the houses they had replaced, and churned out an ill-educated underclass. Even by the late 1960s, it was apparent that the building program had been a social failure. This was what Led Zeppelin wanted to reflect on their new cover, Page explained. "The old man, carrying the wood, is in harmony with nature. He takes from nature and gives back to the land, it's a natural circle. It's right. His old cottage gets pulled down and they put him in these urban slums, terrible places."

Even within the band, however, the cover was open to interpretation. Bonham, possibly the least poetic of the four band members, said, "The cover means whatever people want to read into it. For me, it means I'd rather live in an old house than a block of flats."

The final "mystery" of the outside cover rests with the identity of the old man himself. It has been claimed that he is George Pickingill, a late 19th-century English occultist who counted Aleister Crowley among his pupils. Although the likeness to Pickingill is strong, it seems the image may have come from a more mundane and less significant source. According to Page, Plant found the picture in a junk shop in the town of Reading in Berkshire.

Inside the sleeve was a much more obviously mystical picture—a drawing, by Page's friend Barrington Colby, of an old man standing atop a mountain, holding out a beacon toward which a young man is climbing up the hill. Again, most of the symbolism isn't hard to decipher. The old man standing on the mountain top is the Hermit from the Tarot. In the Tarot, the Hermit is both a seeker and distributor of wisdom. Having found inner fulfillment, he has switched on a light within, the lamp lighting the way for others. But inner fulfillment comes at a price, and the rest of the world is pale and dull to him, monochromatic and unimportant. The road to peace and knowledge is also dangerous, and great self-reliance and self-trust are needed before reaching the light.

To someone like Page, a student of the Tarot and an acknowledged user of the cards, the imagery of the Hermit would have been too much to resist: it was a representation of both the self-belief and self-reliance that he and his band had—and needed to survive. Page also considered himself to be someone leading the young men of his audience (some even suggest the young men of his band) to enlightenment and fulfillment.

Page's knowledge of the Tarot was born out of his infatuation with the occult, and in particular with Aleister Crowley. Crowley was, and probably still is, the most infamous occultist in history. Although he became a pariah in his own time, many of the less extreme philosophies he followed throughout his life have become relatively conventional thought within "new age" circles.

Born in 1875 to a middle-class family, on the surface Crowley was the very model of what Victorian society strove to be. Well educated, questing, and forward-thinking, he was adventurous and daring both mentally and physically. His poems were published while he was still studying at Oxford University, and he was one of the foremost mountaineers of the era.

The turn of any century always prompts an acceleration of sciences, both physical and spiritual. As the current generation rushes to meet its rapidly approaching future, it will of course question the world around itself—what has been achieved, and what could yet still be done before the calendar moves into its next phase. Just as the world saw an unprecedented growth of doomsday cults and new religions in the years leading up to the beginning of the 21st century, the Victorians, too, became fascinated by their own recent history, where they were going in their near future, and how they could turn the knowledge of ancient civilizations to their advantage. The Victorians, for all their ideals of honor and chivalry, were also questers, and it is no coincidence that much of the groundwork for the knowledge we have of, say, ancient Egypt or South American civilizations and their gods and demons, was begun by explorers and archaeologists in the last years of the 19th and first decade of the 20th centuries. It also became fashionable to seek knowledge of the occult sciences.

Aleister Crowley was initially no different from his peers, but he took his interests further than most. Joining a group known as the Hermetic Order of the Golden Dawn, one of the leading occult societies of the day, he sought the knowledge others could pass on to him, but was eventually denied promotion within the Order as his ideas and motives moved beyond those of the organization.

As his personal studies progressed, Crowley became more and more ostracized from polite society. His use of drugs and sex in his spells and incantations became whispered about within the circles that had once welcomed him. Whether spending a year in Mexico trying to make his reflection disappear, holed up in Boleskine House above Loch Ness in the Highlands of Scotland, or at his satanic temple in London, he began styling himself as "The Great Beast 666," a diabolical version of the bright young thing he had once been. He was hounded, and country after country rejected his presence within its borders. In the 1920s he set up the Abbey of Themela in Cefalu, Sicily. In reality the abbey was an old farmhouse where he and his followers indulged in drug-fueled orgies as they tested the boundaries of sanity and human endurance, all in the name of release from earthly morality and mortality.

One former follower who escaped relatively unscathed gave an eyewitness account to the tabloid papers of the day. In one front page report, under the headline "The Wickedest Man in the World," the woman described spells being cast that involved the consumption of mountains of narcotics and, toward the end, as the abbey's residents became saturated and jaded in their own decadence, bestiality. The Italian government, then run by Mussolini, grew tired of the bad press they were getting for allowing Crowley to reside within their borders and ejected him and his followers. Returning to the United Kingdom, Crowley's hold over his followers diminished. Eventually he retired from his quest and died a sad and broken old junkie in Brighton in 1947.

During the 1960s, interest in Crowley increased again, as did an interest in the occult. Rock stars in particular found within the "dark side" an easy path to rebellion, and many became interested in such practices. Heavy metal, in particular, is littered with the imagery of satanism and the occult, but people such as David Bowie went even further: the singer claimed to have witnessed some dark evil swirling in his Los Angeles swimming pool, turning the water black during the middle of the day. The fact that he was out of his mind on cocaine and had barely slept for days may well have influenced his judgment, however.

In recent years, some of Crowley's ideas have been taken up within the New Age movement. Tarot cards are used by so-called mystics in their newspaper columns, reducing the supposed mirror of the soul to a mere parlor game, while part of Crowley's "sex magick," which once scandalized society, has been rebranded as tantric sex and is espoused by the likes of Sting.

Basically, Crowley's philosophy was summed up in his creed: "Do what thou wilt shall be the whole of the law." Roughly translated, it means that there are no moral rules; as long as you're prepared to take the consequences, you are free to do what you want. It's certainly a creed that Jimmy Page and at least two of his fellow band members lived by for much of the 1970s.

Underlying all of Crowley's excesses and scandalous behavior, however, was an altruistic quest to extract the essential truths from all the traditional schools of wisdom and religion, and to unify them in one holistic truth, which he believed would guide modern man through the search for spiritual fulfillment. Such a huge task was, however, beyond even his energies, but it did have one manifestation: Crowley's dramatic and sometimes gaudy rendition of the Tarot. The deck is packed with all the major themes and symbolism from the many previous versions of the Tarot and, in this way, "unites" them. Although they were not published within his lifetime, it is more than likely that these cards were studied and used by Page. The Hermit of Led Zeppelin's album sleeve, however, bears little obvious relation to the more abstract design of Crowley's Tarot. Instead, it is almost a direct copy of a much more widely used deck called the Rider Pack, first published by A. E. Waite in his 1910 book *The Pictorial Key to the Tarot*.

Page's infatuation with Crowley is legendary, and it no doubt contributes greatly to the mythology surrounding Led Zeppelin. Page became interested in mysticism and occultism along with others during its 1960s resurgence. However, like Crowley himself, while his peers merely dabbled and cast it aside, Page took his interest much further. In fact, he has become one of the leading collectors of Crowley artifacts. His obsession even went as far as buying Boleskine House, the distinctly creepy property above Loch Ness that locals still claim is haunted. It was here that Crowley conducted many of his studies, and people claim that it is haunted by the spirits and demons he summoned up during his many black masses. A lodgekeeper went insane at the property during Crowley's ownership, and strange, shadowy figures supposedly shrouded the house while he was in residence. Crowley even wrote that, while he was copying magic symbols, the rooms at the house would become so dark he had to turn on lights during the middle of sunny days. Boleskine is supposedly built on the site of a church that was razed with its entire congregation still inside, so it was never destined to be just any old house long before "The Great Beast 666" arrived on its doorstep.

One other, slightly more sinister and subliminal symbol lies hidden within the picture on the inner sleeve to *Led Zeppelin IV*. If the sleeve is held up to a mirror, with the Hermit's back to the glass, halfway down the rocks of the mountain a vision of a horned bovine beast is revealed. Given the rumors of soul-selling and Page's interest in both Crowley and the occult, the image is unlikely to be a coincidence. Whether it is a serious attempt at subliminal art or an inside-joke by the guitarist and artist Colby, however, is unrecorded, and Page has never offered an explanation of why it is there.

But the main talking point of *Led Zeppelin IV*'s cover is undoubtedly the four symbols that officially name the album. During recording, Page decided that instead of a proper title, the new album would be represented by vaguely mystical runes that were meant to symbolize the individual members of the group.

"Jimmy got the idea not to give the album a name, just to use four symbols," John Paul Jones has explained. "He showed me this book he had, *The Book of Signs* by Rudolph Koch, and said we should all choose a symbol from the book to represent each one of us. So Bonzo and I did this, and it wasn't until much later that we discovered Jimmy and Robert had gone off and had their symbols specially designed for them. Typical, really."

Surprisingly, considering that the images have had such an impact, the rune images appear only once on the original vinyl version of the album's artwork, and even then it's only on the circular label in the middle of the record (the CD reissue included the runes on the spine). In turn, reading from the left, the symbols represent Page ("Zoso"), Jones (a trinity imposed on a circle), Bonham (three interlocked circles), and Plant (a feather inside a circle).

Detailed interpretation of the symbols is virtually impossible without input from the people who chose them, something no member of the band has ever felt the need to do. It is possible to find similar symbols and divine the meaning of those, but even they are open to interpretation. At least it is known where the runes Jones and Bonham chose came from, and so it is reasonable to assume that their meaning closely resembles that suggested by Koch. The sign Bonham chose has three interlocked circles, one at the top and two at the bottom. Although it usually represents the trinity of man, woman, and child—or, if you're Christian, the trinity of Father, Son, and Holy Ghost—it's unlikely that these were the reasons Bonham picked it. Although none of the band have ever been keen to comment on each other's symbols, Page has offered the explanation that Bonham chose it "just because he liked it." Bonham himself was also pleased to note that it was an inversion of the trademark for his favorite American beer, Ballantine.

John Paul Jones also chose a symbol from Koch's book, a rune not dissimilar to that of Bonham. The symbol takes the interlinked part of three circles and puts them against another, smaller circle. One interpretation of the rune, again posited by Page, is that it represents a person of skill and competence, due to it being very difficult to draw accurately. According to Koch, however, the rune was also used, like the pentagram and octogram, to exorcize evil spirits. This use, unsurprisingly, has been taken by the more fringe Zeppelin fans as proof of the theory that Jones alone among the band didn't sell his soul to the Devil, used the symbol as protection against the others, and hence was able to survive within the group relatively unscathed.

Of all four signs, Robert Plant's feather within a circle is probably the least mystical in origin. Throughout many cultures, the feather appears prominently as a sign of courage and truth, and Plant himself has offered just such an explanation for its inclusion in his personal symbol: "The feather is a symbol on which all sorts of philosophies have been based, and it has an interesting heritage. For instance, it means courage to many [Native American] tribes. I like to lay down the truth. No bullshit. That's what the feather in the circle is all about."

This being Led Zeppelin, however—with its fascination for light and dark, simplicity and intricacy—as ever there is another side to Plant's representation. He also claims it is a sacred symbol of the ancient culture of Mu, for which he gives the following explanation: "The Mu civilization existed about 15,000 years ago as part of a lost continent somewhere in the Pacific Ocean between China and Mexico. All sorts of things can be tied in with Mu, even the Easter Island effigies. These Mu people left stone tablets with their symbols inscribed into them all over the place—Mexico, Egypt, India, China, and other places—and they all date from the same period. The Chinese say these people came from the east and the Mexicans say they came from the west, so obviously it was somewhere in between."

The theory of a lost continent is as old as mythology, going back at least as far as Plato and possibly further to another Greek ancient, Solon. In the 1920s and 1930s, Colonel James Churchward wrote books about the fabled lost continent of Mu, a name he purloined from two Frenchmen, claiming that Darwin was wrong and that Mu was the motherland of all mankind. It is not a giant leap to assume that Plant took his feather symbol from within the pages of Churchward's books (even though they are largely regarded as works of fantasy) in which the author claims

detailed knowledge of how the 63 million people who popu-
lated Mu lived. John Macmillan Brown, a former professor
at the University of Canterbury, New Zealand, published a
startling book in 1924 in which he claimed that the whole of
Polynesia was once a vast continent, the only remnants of
which now form most of the islands dotted throughout the
Pacific Ocean. This theory, and similar ones, are taken by
many as the starting point for believing Mu really existed.

The most obvious other rock manifestation of Mu is in the
stadium dance act formed in the 1980s by British musicians
Bill Drummond and Jimmy Cauty, variously called the
Timelords, the JAMS, the KLF (Kopyright Liberation Front),
and the Justified Ancients of Mu Mu. Drummond and Cauty,
as famous for their scams and early championing of sampling
as for their music, took their Mu moniker from the *Illuminatus!*
Trilogy, a book cowritten by arch futurist, conspiracy theorist
and, apparently, New Age stand-up comedian Robert Anton
Wilson. In it the Mu are the remnants of the civilization of
Atlantis. Dreaded enemies of the Illuminati, they are dedicated to chaos, disruption, and the ultimate downfall of
world order—not unlike Drummond and Cauty themselves.

By far the most complicated and esoteric symbol of the
four belongs, of course, to Page. Because the guitarist is a follower of the occult (and even a former owner of his own
occult bookshop, the Equinox, which shared its name with a
periodical once published by a Mr. A. Crowley) this sign has
come to represent the album more than any other. Many
people call it by the letters it most closely resembles: Zoso.

Although he has never publicly explained the meaning of
the symbol, Page has claimed it as his own design: "A lot of

people mistook it for a word—Zoso—which is a pity, because it wasn't supposed to be a word at all, but something entirely different."

The only clue to its meaning that Page has ever offered is "Thursday," which is a scant and unsatisfying explanation by anyone's terms. It does, however, provide a starting point. Thursday on our calendar is named after the Norse god Thor, who—as any reader of Marvel Comics will know—wielded a hammer as the defender of the world. As pointed out by Led Zeppelin biographer Robert Godwin, Thor is also analogous with the Roman god Jupiter, and the "Z" part of the symbol can be linked to both gods: the letter "Z" represents Jupiter's lightning bolt, while the underscoring tail contains the "T" which represents Thor's hammer. In interviews, members of the band have referred to Led Zeppelin's sound as that of "the hammer of the gods," hence the title of Stephen Davis's biography of the band (from a lyric in Led Zeppelin III's "Immigrant Song"). Godwin, who has obviously undertaken considerable research into the subject, also claims that an old alchemical text contains elements of Page's symbol, a Z with a line through the middle which has filled in circles on each end—not dissimilar to the linked part of Zoso. This symbol, too, represents Jupiter and Thor.

Godwin goes further in drawing connections with the Rosicrucian Order which, although inconclusive, nevertheless provide easily traceable links back to Page. The order, which traces its lineage back to ancient Egypt, pursued intellectual ideals they believed to be found within ancient symbols and texts. They even claimed Solon, the ancient Greek who posited the theory of a lost, sunken continent, among their earliest members. Many groups splintered off from the Rosicrucians in the 19th century, among them the Hermetic Order of the Golden Dawn, founded by high-ranking Freemasons in 1888 and the organization Crowley once belonged to. Another splinter group was the Theosophical Society, founded in 1875 in New York by Russian Helene Blavatsky, who wrote at least one book containing a detailed description of the lost continent of Lemuria, which manifests itself in other mystical orders as Atlantis and, indeed, Mu.

The only time Page allegedly offered an explanation of his symbol was to Plant alone. According to Plant, "You may not believe this, but Pagey once took me aside and said, 'Look, I'm going to tell you this once and then I shan't ever mention it again, or at least not for a very long time.' And would you believe that I've since forgotten what it was, and now Pagey won't tell me. That's the only light I can throw on it."

Whatever the significance of the symbols, to those who picked them and to those who try to divine their meanings (and there is no real proof that they even represent each member of the band, rather than being one complete symbol in itself), what they represented most was a club that the fans could join—a secret society, as Stephen Davis has put it. Here was mysticism writ large across the very face of the greatest album by the biggest band in the world, and yet only those who "knew," or had smoked enough dope, could begin to fathom the depths of its mysteries and meanings. A Led Zeppelin society had indeed finally gelled. It had been a ragtag bunch before, but now it came together around the twin totems of the four symbols and its very own anthem, "Stairway to Heaven."

that's the way: track by track

It starts with the sound of an amplifier warming up and ends, just over 42 minutes later, having turned music as much on its head as *Sgt. Pepper's Lonely Hearts Club Band* had four years earlier. Nothing before had sounded like Led Zeppelin's fourth album, and very little would manage to sound quite like it again for years. Such was the economy of the album, the density of the production, that a whole new dynamic approach to white blues was invented. Add in the mystical rumors and disinformation that surrounded the group and you had the blueprint for every future metal band's first rehearsal. Everyone would strive to recreate what Led Zeppelin somehow managed with almost unseemly ease, but everyone else was doomed to get it ever so slightly wrong for ever more—even Led Zeppelin itself.

Of course, there had been groundbreaking albums before. Although *Sgt. Pepper's Lonely Hearts Club Band* threw down a visionary gauntlet to every other band of the time, the Beatles had really made their quantum leap with 1966's *Revolver*, forever releasing them from their "loveable mop top" sobriquet and leaving them little other place to go than too far, which really is where *Sgt. Pepper* went. With *Let It Bleed* in 1969, the Rolling Stones stopped trying to be the Beatles and embraced the drugged-out bad-boy blues that led directly to the morphine pop of *Sticky Fingers*, but then went too far on the comparatively somnambulant *Exile on Main Street*. Brian Wilson's 1967 magnum opus *Pet Sounds* left the boy genius all but paralyzed with self-doubt and paranoia, finally sending him so over the top when he tried to record its successor, *Smile*, that the album would never receive an official release and only came out in dribs and drabs over the following 25 years. Even Jimi Hendrix's wigged-out space-rock debut *Are You Experienced* tied him up in knots, having already taken him further than he would ever go again. So, too, Led Zeppelin could only go so far before repeating their own formula in ever decreasing circles.

Each of the first three albums, although differing wildly from one another, had an internal stylistic cohesion, and *Led Zeppelin II* and *III* were each a vast progression from their predecessor. Few people could see exactly what was unfolding in front of the band, and perhaps it is only with hindsight that anyone could be expected to see the whole picture. Most groups' debuts are made up of their best tracks, accumulated over years of touring and road-tested on countless live audiences. However, almost the first thing that Led Zeppelin did as a band was record an album. Here was a band with almost no history before its debut album, a band finding its feet and style in public. In the time it takes most acts to get signed, Led Zeppelin had recorded three platinum albums and was working on its fourth. Most groups play for years before getting near a studio, but Jimmy Page's wealth (Peter Grant won their huge advance, but Page paid for the debut) allowed them to go straight to step six of the rock handbook without having to rely on a record company's backing.

Although powerful and gripping, *Led Zeppelin I* is nonetheless the sound of a group introducing themselves to each other, and is very much a Page solo album that features an inspired backing band. By *Led Zeppelin II*, recorded over the next eight months, ideas from the other members were starting to come through. John Paul Jones was gaining confidence and putting forward his arrangement ideas, but the biggest leap was coming from Robert Plant, who was starting to flourish as a lyricist. On the first album he had written very few lyrics—there was no time to write any—and the tracks that weren't covers or adaptations of traditional blues songs were left over from Page's Yardbirds days. *Led Zeppelin II's* "What Is and What Should Never Be" and "Ramble On" particularly highlighted Plant's growing talent, and the singer himself has cited his writing of "Ramble On" as the first time he felt truly satisfied with a lyric, the first time he felt he had written something that projected both himself and where he wanted to go musically. *Led Zeppelin III* was very much the Page and Plant show in full effect, but again, there was little time to develop musically, aside from testing the waters to see how far they could take the acoustic side of their music without losing their essential power.

Hoary old blues riffs such as those on their debut album could obviously never contain a band made up of very musically ambitious members (with the possible exception of Bonham, who focused solely on drumming). Marrying those riffs to the orgasmic bombast of *Led Zeppelin II* worked in terms of sales, but again was hardly stretching them anywhere near as far as they could go. The lightness of *Led Zeppelin III*, which breathed air into the creative lungs of the band after the dark roar of the second album, was, in hindsight, merely a stepping stone to something even more daring in breadth and scope. Peeved at the critics' lack of understanding about what they were trying to achieve, Led Zeppelin pushed themselves as never before.

Black Dog

From those starting sounds of Jimmy Page warming up his amp, "Black Dog," the first track on *Led Zeppelin IV*, ushers in a new confidence that leads the band, for the first time, way beyond the sum of its parts. It's a bruising, hammering opening track even by Led Zeppelin's standards, with Plant's wailing yowl leading to Page's sometimes triple-tracked guitars. The whole thing burns along a riff brought to the Headley Grange sessions by John Paul Jones, that was inspired by Muddy Waters's 1968 *Electric Mud* album, an uncommon place to find inspiration.

Although a giant not only of the blues but of all 20th century music, Waters (born McKinley Morganfield) was encouraged by Chess Records to adapt his aggressive Chicago blues—a genre he pioneered when he arrived in the Windy City in the 1940s—to take in a more "Jimi Hendrix," psychedelic approach. Hence *Electric Mud*. The record company men thought it would sell their artist to a new, white audience, but it flopped. It has since been championed by such groundbreaking DJs as David Holmes, however, and critics now claim that it was a crucial forebear to the psychedelic soul of the 1970s, marrying Waters's delta blues roots to fuzzed-up wah-wah solos, echoes of which can obviously be heard in "Black Dog." Page and Plant later made their debt to

Waters even more obvious by naming their 1998 album *Walking into Clarksdale*, after the town in which the great bluesman grew up.

Ever the arranger, Jones decreed that "Black Dog" couldn't be too simple and had to switch back on itself, creating a deceptively complex song. One of the song's less likely cover versions is by the Hampton String Quartet, a group of New York Juilliard School of Music graduates who specialize in, unsurprisingly, string quartet versions of rock songs. According to their main arranger, John Reid, the song is one of the most complex he has ever had to score. "When I listened to 'Black Dog'," Reid says, "I was amazed by the complexity. It has something like 98 time signature changes and is the most difficult of any song we play. If any of our regular members can't perform, it is the one song we have to drop from the set—which is a shame, because it's usually our opening number—as there is no way that someone can just come in and learn it off the sheet music. It's something you have to play to understand."

This complexity tested Page's skills as a producer to the limit. For years, he had watched the top producers of the 1960s at work in the studio. Rather than sitting on his ass doing nothing or playing darts in the studio lounge, Page soaked up whatever information he could, making mental notes of how he would do it differently when he got to sit in the producer's chair. He also had long-standing friendships with young engineers Glyn Johns, an old acquaintance from Epsom, and Eddie Kramer, who would work by his side on the first and the second albums respectively. From the outset, Page had always intended to produce Led Zeppelin. Prior to forming the band, he had been a house producer of sorts for Andrew Loog Oldham's Immediate label, taking charge of sessions for Chris Farlowe and a pre-Velvet Underground Nico, as well as John Mayall's Bluesbreakers (which at the time featured Eric Clapton, who had recently departed from the Yardbirds).

Page was hardly a proven commodity behind the desk, however. Even so, he and Peter Grant had thought through Led Zeppelin's contract demands very carefully, and Atlantic was specifically denied any say over prospective producers. Besides, by the time the band signed with the label the first album was already in the can, and even Atlantic wasn't going to mess with the formula that presented them with the hottest new group in town.

Page has never received much credit for his production abilities, but it is those very talents that attract people like Black Crowes' guitarist Rich Robinson to his work. In 1999 the Black Crowes played an entire tour with Page, eventually releasing an album of Led Zeppelin songs, *Live at the Greek*, from that tour. Robinson and his brother Chris, the Black Crowes' singer—both massive Led Zeppelin fans from an early age—had jumped at the chance of playing with one of their heroes at a benefit gig the year before, and they suggested to the guitarist that they continue with the collaboration. Standing onstage alongside his hero, Robinson says he was particularly inspired to take his own playing to another level. "Standing there," he said, "you know that you're standing beside Jimmy Page. No one else plays the way he does, there is no one else like him, no one who was so passionate or so great. It's like playing with Michael Jordan or Tiger Woods."

Even so, Robinson says that he was never daunted playing alongside someone without whom his own band could never have existed, as it wasn't Page's guitar playing that initially drew him to Led Zeppelin. "I've never really been one for idolizing people. I love the way Jimmy plays guitar, but it was the way he put things together that really interested me. I never bought into the mysticism of Robert's lyrics, but the way he used his voice—the way Jimmy layered that voice onto the melody and mixed it into the rest of the music again creates something that had never been done before and, particularly on *Led Zeppelin IV*, it went much further than anyone else ever took that amalgamation. He was often accused of ripping old blues guys off, but he never did. If you listen to Duane Allman, now he really was ripping them off, but Jimmy came from a whole different area. He combined so many different things, it was like classical music—the way he orchestrated it in a bombastic kind of way, taking beautiful chords and adding these blues scale licks alongside."

Lyrically, "Black Dog" is fairly straightforward, dealing with the classic blues theme of, basically, a woman turning bad on the protagonist. After the initial euphemisms of great, wanton sex ("Watch your honey drip/can't keep away"), the singer proclaims that the woman is "a wrong 'un". Eventually he learns his lesson that "a big-legged woman ain't got no soul." Considering Plant's extensive knowledge of groupies during the early years of Led Zeppelin, it seems only fair that one of them might have gotten one over on him for a change.

An interesting and contemporaneous version of the song appears on the *BBC Sessions* album released in 1997. Ultimately not broadcast, this version—which marked one of the first times the song had been played to an audience—sounded almost jolly during the guitar breaks punctuating the lines of the verses and climaxed with a final solo by Page that is the equal of any of the offerings of today's garage punks for its scratchy, rusty, and outright raw edge. The traditional blues nature of the lyric is further enhanced by Plant's vocal delivery, which is deliberately distorted to sound like the early recordings of his black heroes. Obvious echoes of the overall effect can be heard in such recent artists as the White Stripes.

Rock and Roll

Page's production abilities aside, track two, "Rock and Roll," was driven by a very different kind of musician—John Bonham. Although he was never the sharpest knife in the musical drawer, Bonham had an unbeatable raw talent that kept him at the very heart of the band. "Rock and Roll" was one of the first Led Zeppelin songs instigated by its drummer, who started bashing out the rhythm in frustration at not being able to master the pattern of "Four Sticks." Page spontaneously joined in on a riff, and suddenly the whole song was there, with Plant inventing the lyric—yearning for the old days of no nonsense rock 'n' roll music—virtually on the spot. The result is a rollicking, raw, blasting boogie number that hangs on Bonham's drumming. His flair was as much for what he left out as what he put in, and the tension in "Rock and Roll," as with most Zeppelin songs with a heavy drum beat, was brought about by his natural little skips and flams.

Without Bonham, the band would never have sounded as they did, and they may well have been mere also-rans. It's an impression borne out by the fact that, when Bonham died in 1980, the band barely had to consider the question of whether to continue without him. What he brought to the mix was a natural rhythmic feel that went beyond merely keeping time. He wanted and strived for drumming that, like Plant's vocals, became a part of the fabric of a song's melody, and, from his earliest days behind a kit, he worked toward his goal. Such was his innate talent that he seldom practised after Led Zeppelin was formed; they were so rarely off the road or not recording in their first three years that he didn't need to. Later, he would be so drink- and drug-soaked that he rarely felt the urge to play when off the road. And yet so immersed was he in what he did that he barely thought about how it was achieved.

"Feeling is a lot more important than technique," he told one interviewer. "It's all very well playing a triple paradiddle, but who's going to know you're doing it?"

The force with which Bonham hit his kit flattered to deceive and, although he is the idol of every metal drummer since, none have been able to match his deft touch. What truly sets his work aside is the flick that went with the power, the ability to whip the stick off the drumhead at the very point it landed, making even the most bog-standard four-time rock rhythm swing.

The other skill that set Bonham apart was his untutored (for that matter, unteachable) internal balance. Most drummers have a heavy foot on the kick drum, a particular snatch off the snare, or even a quickness around the toms that engineers compensate for by miking up the kit in such a way as to balance it out in the mixing. Bonham didn't need such frippery. On much of his recorded work, certainly through-out most of the recording of *Led Zeppelin IV*, he had one mic for the entire kit. Apart from the very occasional bit of compression or echo, what you get on this album is exactly what he played. That is something that other "star" drummers such as Keith Moon, Ginger Baker, and even Mötley Crüe's Tommy Lee, one of the most obviously Bonham-influenced metal sticksmen, would never be able to boast of. But "Rock and Roll" was hardly the drumming acme of this particular offering: that wouldn't come until the album's very end.

The Battle of Evermore

After the helter-skelter pace and roaring rock of the opening tracks, the album's third song, "The Battle of Evermore," couldn't be more different. From their earliest days, Page and Plant had considered the notion of recording modern English folk songs in much the same style as Pentangle or the Incredible String Band. Though they had nodded toward such influences previously, most notably on *Led Zeppelin III*, nothing had gone quite this far before. Although it may be one of the more dated-sounding tracks on the album, the band never felt embarrassed by it, even though it, along with its more grown-up sibling, "Stairway to Heaven," is largely responsible for much of the wizards and demons nonsense that many metal bands felt compelled to record in its wake.

Remove it from such historical context, however, and you are left with a pretty English folk ballad that tells the tale of a walled city under siege. Plant had always been fascinated by the wars England fought with its mainland neighbors, Scotland and Wales, and he'd been reading about the

Scottish wars and writing lyrics that vaguely pertained to his recent reading. He also revisited the lyrical territory of J.R.R. Tolkien's *The Lord of the Rings* (references to which had most notably appeared earlier in *Led Zeppelin II*'s "Ramble On") and came up with a call-and-response playlet, sung with Sandy Denny. Thirty odd years since its release, however, the song has been polluted by its own success in giving rise to some of the most atrocious heavy metal and progressive rock ever foisted on an audience. Some bands, including Yes, Marillion, Uriah Heep, Rainbow, and, more recently, lesser acts such as Ozric Tentacles, have created not just albums out of such themes, but entire careers.

The song was revived in a very different form for the 1994 album *No Quarter: Jimmy Page and Robert Plant Unledded*. On the album, recorded for MTV as part of its *Unplugged* series, Page and Plant sought to find the ultimate mix of Led Zeppelin and the eastern musical styles with which they had experimented in the 1970s, here employing Egyptian and Indian musicians to play alongside traditional rockers.

To this end, instead of replacing Denny with a similar traditional folk vocalist, the duo acquired the services of British-born Indian singer Najma Akhtar, herself a pioneering musician. (Akhtar had upset purists in the late 1980s when she combined western harmonies with the northern Indian *ghazal* music of her ancestral home.) The result sounded more like something you'd hear in an Indian bazaar or Moroccan souk. Its only rival on the *No Quarter* album, in terms of an effortless blending of eastern and western styles, is "Kashmir," the track from *Physical Graffiti* that had always folded these influences into each other. Strangely, even the Tolkienderived lyrical stylings of "The Battle of Evermore" sound fresh presented in this new light. Perhaps Led Zeppelin was right to never be embarrassed by the song.

Stairway to Heaven

A similar fate has, sadly, also become attached to the jewel in the crown, "Stairway to Heaven." Led Zeppelin's touchstone track has, over the years, gone from inspirational youth anthem to the very epitome of bloated rock excess and back to readily accepted classic (even if it has been adopted with no little sense of irony by a more recent audience). But the fact is that the song has been diminished by endless imitations, and it is almost impossible to listen to it with fresh, clean ears. Such is its stature and success: if people know one thing about Led Zeppelin, it's that they are "the 'Stairway to Heaven' band." When *Led Zeppelin IV* was released, it was "Stairway to Heaven" that critics pointed to as the undisputed centerpiece of the album—and the song that the fans wanted to hear more than any other.

So what is it that draws people to the song again and again after all these years? One reason is the sublime music. From the gentlest of picked six-string openings, with Jones's recorders tracked over the top, it slowly progresses through an ever-steepening ascent as electric guitars and, finally, Bonham's drums enter the fray—much later than any other group at the time would have dared. The tension it creates is astounding; everything is held back until the last possible moment. And when the guitar solo finally kicks in and all that tension explodes, it goes still further, Bonham's furious machine-gun fills pushing along the pace.

Its beginning is matched by a yearning lyric of longing and questing—the universal subject of desire. Although the woman in the song may have the wrong idea about how to achieve her quest—by buying the titular stairway—it's still something that everyone can relate to, an innate need in almost all humans to strive for more than they have, be it spiritual or material. This is where, more than in any song, Led Zeppelin's personal philosophies and interests combine, particularly Page's occult interests and Plant's down-to-earth hippie ideals.

Although Atlantic insisted on releasing first "Black Dog" and then "Rock and Roll" as U.S. singles, neither performed the way the company had hoped. What they were really holding out for was "Stairway to Heaven" as a single. In 1971, Top 40-based AM radio was the king in the United States, and the natural way to promote any album of the time. Even though it was only an album track, and an eight-minute long album track at that, some more progressive stations had begun playing "Stairway to Heaven" already. Not wanting to miss out on any cash that could be milked from its star act, Atlantic begged Peter Grant for permission to make it an official single release. Grant refused, in spite of the fact that, as was pointed out by Atlantic, there were already advance orders of 100,000 copies, even though it hadn't even been manufactured. Grant stood fast on the subject in spite of Atlantic's increasingly urgent requests. History was to show the manager to be wilier than people had yet imagined.

Because they couldn't buy "Stairway to Heaven" as a single, fans had to buy the album, which generated even higher financial returns for all involved. The extent to which people bought *Led Zeppelin IV* just for "Stairway to Heaven" is illustrated by the story of the 10-millionth album. In the mid-1980s, as sales of *IV* approached the milestone, it was to be marked by the awarding of a "diamond disc." Atlantic contrived a scam to give a brooch made of diamond and gold to the purchaser of the mystical 10-millionth copy to roll off the pressing line. Notification of the prize-winning purchase was via a secret message mastered in between two songs on side two: "Four Sticks" and "Going to California." In spite of heavy publicity (it was supposedly a one-carat diamond and therefore rather worth collecting), it was two years before a Canadian woman finally claimed her prize. She had only bought the album for "Stairway to Heaven" and had never gotten around to listening to the second side.

Not everyone is a fan of the song, however, and it has received an incredible amount of criticism, particularly from fundamentalist religious groups. Their problem? Back-masking. Ever since products have been promoted, people have been wary of subliminal messages in their media. One famous example of this practice is a study conducted in the 1950s, in which the words "Eat popcorn, drink Coke" were flashed on screen for a third of a millisecond every five seconds during the showing of a movie—too quickly for the human eye to register its appearance, but possibly long enough for the subconscious to notice. The man conducting the study, James Vicary, reported that Coke sales went up 18 percent, and that popcorn consumption increased by 58 percent. The result was the passing of laws forbidding the use of such "blipvert" advertising, but rumors of its insidious presence abounded. In the 1970s the word "sex" was supposedly hidden within ice cubes on a billboard advertisement for Gilbeys Gin. The theory was that anyone seeing the poster would become aroused, thus making the product more memorable. But, most pernicious of all, rock musicians were rumored to hide Satanic messages within their music, secret exhortations that could only be discovered if the record was played backward.

Led Zeppelin, because of its enormous success and the well-known taste for the occult enjoyed by its leader, was always going to be a target for such rumors. In 1982 a Southern Baptist minister claimed on his TV show that he had discovered Satanic messages hidden within "Stairway to Heaven." Picking up on the allegations, a California politician informed the state assembly that there were no less than nine such messages on the song, among them "I will sing because I live with Satan" and "I love Satan"— phrases that religious zealots believed would corrupt an innocent and unsuspecting youth, leading them to Satan's very door.

Leaving aside the rather poor faith these people have in their apparently dim-witted children's ability to think for themselves, as well as the question of whether or not these phrases actually exist on the album, studies into the effectiveness of backmasking have cast doubts on people's ability to discern or be affected by such messages. In 1985 psychologists J. Vokey and J. D. Read conducted a study using Psalm 23, Queen's "Another One Bites the Dust," and various other passages made up especially for the experiment. Of the people tested, few could hear any message. When prompted to listen for a particular phrase, however, 90 percent were able to hear it. Vokey and Read concluded that if backmasking did indeed exist, it was ineffective. Their volunteers had trouble even noticing the backmasked phrase when the tape was played forward, were unable to judge the type of message (whether it was Christian, Satanic, or commercial) it contained, and weren't led to behave in any certain way as a result of being "exposed" to the backmasked phrases.

Backmasking *does* exist, nevertheless, and it has been used by bands, including Electric Light Orchestra and Pink Floyd, to leave joke messages for fans to discover should they have too much time on their hands. The Beatles unintentionally left a backward message on their song "Rain" after a mistake in the studio; John Lennon just liked the sound of backward gibberish on the song. Whether these or any other instances of backmasking have been perpetrated for nefarious purposes, and whether or not they corrupt anyone unfortunate enough to hear them, it's fair to say that no amount of scientific study casting doubt on its success rate is going to convince people who want to believe that Satan himself puts the messages on rock records without help from either the record companies or, indeed, the band itself.

Newspapers around the world picked up the backmasking story. As the accusations flew, Led Zeppelin's Swan Song record label issued a terse statement, its lone comment on the subject: "Our turntables only play in one direction."

And anyway, as Rich Robinson says, "Stairway to Heaven sounds so amazing played forward why the fuck would anyone want to play it backward?" It's hard to argue with him.

Misty Mountain Hop

Compared to the tempestuous first side of the album, side two of *Led Zeppelin IV* is a relatively straightforward affair.

Opening with "Misty Mountain Hop," a dense, fuzzed blues riff that is a distant cousin of "Rock and Roll," it starts with bouncing piano and yet another swinging drum beat. Though probably the lightest track on the album, it still showcases the depth that Bonham brought to the band, making a very basic rock pattern slide along hypnotically.

The song also features Plant's only lyrics to deal specifically with drugs, telling the tale of meeting hippies in a park and sharing their dope. Although two alleged incidents are each credited with inspiring the song (a chance meeting in a San Francisco park and a Hyde Park love-in), Plant was in either case making a political point, something Led Zeppelin rarely did. Even in interviews, the group members seldom went further than vague hippie statements about society. The lyric of "Misty Mountain Hop" reflects Plant's quest for a better society, a place and time when hangups are replaced with individual freedom and a life of mutual support and rapport. The one subject that Plant did get on a hobby-horse about was marijuana, particularly the laws governing its use. He was even photographed, pre-Led Zeppelin, at a Midlands' "pro-cannabis" rally in 1968. The picture appeared on the back page of the U.K. *Daily Mail*.

Four Sticks

Apart from its phenomenal drumming, "Four Sticks" is often dismissed as the album's weakest song, and if such an "accolade" has to be awarded, this remarkable track would probably have to take the gong. The song is most remarkable for its strange time signatures and switches, which seem almost an exercise in making a rock tune as complex as possible. But it does highlight an often overlooked psyche-delic aspect of Led Zeppelin's music. The combination of the hypnotic drumming and droning vocals and guitar, plus Jones's early use of a synthesizer, produce a slice of psyche-delia to rival the best acid rock of the late 1960s.

Going to California

A very different kind of 1960s is visited in "Going to California." A tribute to quintessential Californian singer-songwriter Joni Mitchell, the girl "with love in her eyes and flowers in her hair," it's also a wistful paean to Led Zeppelin's spiritual home, the place the band regarded as their own theme park. It's as lovely a song as Led Zeppelin ever record-ed, lilting along on Page's acoustic six-string, with Jones plucking away on the mandolin.

When the Levee Breaks

The final track on the album, "When the Levee Breaks," is possibly Led Zeppelin's second-most influential song ever. It's a crunching, head-crushing tune, a rewrite of a 1928 blues song by Memphis Minnie (1897-1973). Born Lizzie Douglas in Memphis, Tennessee, Minnie was one of the few women blues artists of any era. Like Muddy Waters, she took her music north to Chicago and managed to gain the respect of her male peers, often playing them off the stage. Today she is regarded as one of the finest blues players of her generation, regardless of gender.

"When the Levee Breaks" goes even further in the psy-chedelic stakes than "Four Sticks," its phased guitars and backward loops and echo on the harmonica replicating the phased vision usually experienced during acid trips. Although Led Zeppelin has rarely been associated with psychedelic drugs, it would have been hard for any musician who moved in their circles in the late 1960s to have avoided such temptations. More than cocaine—which was still a relatively new drug on the rock scene at the time—or heroin, LSD was what set the "turned on" world apart from the straight world, giving those who indulged the knowledge that they could detach themselves completely from everything around them.

Apart from its mysterious ability to transport the user into another world, it also breaks down the ego of the user, something that appealed to many musicians of the day. John Lennon in particular spent months at his home, gobbling huge quantities of LSD for the very purpose of losing his ego, while actor Peter Fonda took so much that he once whispered into Lennon's ear that he knew "what it's like to be dead," a statement that freaked the Beatle out for months.

But more important, "When the Levee Breaks" helped give rise to an entire genre of music, and it is John Bonham's true legacy to the world. Even at the earliest rap block parties where DJs mixed records together, "When the Levee Breaks" was used as the beat of choice when you wanted power more than anything else. As the sophistication of mixing evolved and samples started to be used in the studio, that crashing "boom-tcsh, boom-boom-tcsh" (so recognizable as Bonham's) was cut up and grafted onto endless hip hop tracks. The irony is that Led Zeppelin was constantly accused of ripping off black blues music when they started, and now the whole trip had finally come full circle.

It wasn't until record companies found a way of selling hip hop to a white audience, however, that the phenomenon took off. When producer Rick Rubin found a way of keeping both the original power of the drumming and its swing, he made the Beastie Boys famous. In 1986 the opening track of their album *Licensed to Ill*, "Rhymin' & Stealin'," did just that, beginning with the unmistakable opening drums from "When the Levee Breaks." The song, and the album, turned hip hop on its head, finally opening up the genre to a massive white audience and creating the bedrock for all subsequent acts that followed in the Beastie Boys' footsteps. The simple fact is that without Bonham and "When the Levee Breaks," there would be no hip hop as we know it. Since then Bonham's drum track has become one of the two most sampled in history, along with "Funky Drummer" by James Brown.

Asked in Q magazine what Led Zeppelin thought of the beat being so widely used, Plant was philosophical: "We were flabbergasted and impressed when people started using 'When the Levee Breaks.' When Jimmy and I talked about it, we figured nothing was sacred, as we'd been nicking old blues stuff since the beginning of time. It got a bit preposterous when Michael Jackson did 'Bad'—which is the riff to 'Heartbreaker' [from *Led Zeppelin II*] with one note changed and as far as we're concerned is a nick."

Led Zeppelin IV is as strong a collection of individual songs as the band ever recorded. Their three previous albums had struggled to encompass and contain the band's myriad styles and influences, but here the tracks conveyed the full breadth of their ideas with an economy they'd never before managed, resulting in a sleek cohesion at which they had before only hinted. There is no flab here, no make-weight tracks to fill out the grooves. Where their later albums became meandering (*Houses of the Holy* had progressive-rock pretentions; *Physical Graffiti* was a double album fleshed out by off-cuts from the *II, III,* and *IV* sessions; *Presence* was an exercise in technology; and *In Through the Out Door* was a John Paul Jones album that was backed by the rest of the band), *Led Zeppelin IV* was the musical definition of efficacy.

Even the sequencing of the album gives it a dynamic few of their peers could hope for. The headlong rush of "Black Dog" and "Rock and Roll" give way to the calm oasis of "The Battle of Evermore" and "Stairway to Heaven," before side two presents yet another, more playful facet of the group. The sequencing, however, whether by design or accident, also gives the album the feel of a live concert. It's the air guitarist's perfect set list for a quick bedroom-mirror gig: two rampaging numbers to get the heart racing, followed by a couple of slower, more reflective songs from contrast, and finally, the meat of the set, which allows for showing off some virtuoso shapes and finishing with a punishing flourish that leaves you breathless.

Little is known of how Led Zeppelin arrived at the track listing, although it seems that the tracks are pretty much presented in the order they were completed at Headley Grange. If this is the case, it's a far cry from the modern science of sequencing that bands employ today. Radiohead, for example, drove themselves to distraction trying to figure out the song order for its landmark album, *OK Computer*. The band had all just been presented with minidisc players, then cutting-edge technology. Using these machines, listeners can change the order of the songs on an album at the touch of a button, a huge step forward from the unwieldy recording equipment in the studios of the 1970s. Radiohead's singer, Thom Yorke, in particular, claims to have nearly given himself a breakdown by endlessly fiddling with the track listing.

More than anything, *Led Zeppelin IV* is the sound of a band at the peak of its powers. Rushing to prove to the world that they were deserving of their success, the adulation of their fans, and the respect of their contemporaries, Led Zeppelin finally found the sound it had been looking for all along. And the sound was sex. Wherever you look on *IV* (and, to a lesser extent, on the albums leading up to it), sex is the overriding theme, much as it was with the band themselves.

In hindsight, it's easy to look at Led Zeppelin's entire recorded work and see the first two albums as being where the band was coming from before a light was switched on that took them to another place. The third album opened a new door, and *Led Zeppelin IV* explored the room to which it led. Its mixture of sex, drugs, and black magic is a potent force, one that was to earn ridicule from many of the people they sought to impress, but one which a teenage audience of any generation is unlikely to forget. With tales of predatory, soulless big-legged women and waifish hippie girls ready to supply you with drugs and exotic sexual knowledge, the album spelled danger and mystery, a fantasy of infinite pleasure and excess only the privileged rock star, with his ability to step outside the normal moral confines of society, could fulfill. All these things would appear on each of their subsequent albums, but for sheer invention, intuition, and creative ability, nothing in the genre would ever match *Led Zeppelin IV*.

communication breakdown: Led Zeppelin and the press

In 1971 the world was, by today's standards, naive and even quaint, and so were both the music and media industries. Pick up any magazine or newspaper from the period, and it's obvious that mainstream culture largely detested rock music and everything it stood for, while rock music detested the mainstream and all its outdated concerns. The magazines that did cover rock were still very much underground publications. Indeed, rock culture itself was still in its infancy, and it was here that the strong link between music and the media that represented it was forged, forever fudging the dividing line between the publishing and record industries.

During the 1950s and 1960s, music magazines had been benign entities, diligently chronicling tour dates and new releases. It was very much a teen-oriented industry that reflected the tastes of mainstream music programs such as *American Bandstand* in the United States, and *6.5 Special* and *Ready Steady Go!* in the United Kingdom. Magazines were seen as a PR tool for the record labels and they rarely reported with any depth or insight beyond the bass player's favorite color and whether he was currently "seeing anyone special."

As the music grew more sophisticated, however, so did the fans. They demanded more than *Teen Beat* could or would offer them and so an underground press slowly filled the void. Magazines such as the *Village Voice, Rolling Stone,* and *Creem* began covering music as an art form rather than a pastime to be grown out of and discarded when more adult concerns took over the silly, frivolous lives of teenagers. Here was a soundtrack to rebellion and social change, something that was uniquely of its generation and that set that generation apart from all others that had gone before. Music had, through Bob Dylan and the Beatles especially, come to speak for millions who seldom before had a voice to articulate its concerns and demand for change.

As the fans demanded more clarification and elaboration from the artists, so too music journalism grew and developed into a legitimate form of writing to service that demand. Some artists rose to the challenge, seeing it as a way to further communicate their ideas with a wider public than those who bought their records, while others, like Dylan, sought only to obfuscate, speaking in indecipherable code and playing games with the media.

Whichever way bands chose to deal with ever-deeper probing from the best of this new breed of journalist, the cat-and-mouse game become more sophisticated, and the fans lapped it up. The confidence and abilities of journalists grew. So did their egos. Eventually, some came to see themselves as the guardians of a musical moral high ground, arbiters of taste who handed out brickbats if they deemed a band to be less than genuine in its pursuit of artistic integrity. It was exactly at the moment when the underground press was at its most pious and hypocritically solemn that Led Zeppelin entered the fray.

Led Zeppelin and the press never saw eye to eye. While most musicians have a love-hate relationship with the media, the antagonism between Led Zeppelin and the press, particularly the music press, went way beyond the norm. Such was the press's paranoia about Led Zeppelin that the band was never given its due respect and its importance was constantly trivialized. Every band believes that it is due greater respect, and that it is misunderstood by the press. But with Led Zeppelin, it went deeper.

Even signing with Atlantic (for that record $200,000 advance) galled members of the press who decided that they smelled a rat. In their eyes, here was a band with no proven track record signing for a huge advance and with a record company contract that gave them full control over everything. The word "hype" was on everyone's lips. To mock the accusations, Jimmy Page called his song publishing company Superhype. The press failed to get the joke, and instead saw it as yet another indication that the band were money-makers who were selling out their audience.

Led Zeppelin's members didn't understand what they had done. Business was business; all they were doing was letting Peter Grant make sure they got their dues. And to attack their music was unfathomable to this most egotistical of groups. In the beginning, they couldn't understand criticism that they were ripping off the old blues artists. When the Rolling Stones did it, they were hailed as kings who were resurrecting careers of all-but-forgotten musical innovators, but the members of Led Zeppelin were somehow opportunists for daring to elaborate on the formula rather than merely repeating it. When they attempted to answer the criticism by showing a different, more considered, truly original side of the band, they were criticized for dumping their blues roots. When, on *Led Zeppelin IV*, they combined the two, out came the critics' beating stick again, this time to accuse them of marrying their influences into something cynical and—horror—possibly even successful.

And so the media attacked these interlopers. The arbiters of "real" music dismissed the band as a flash in the pan and its audience as stoned teenagers who knew nothing of the finer points of music. Never mind that their first three albums all went into the upper reaches of the charts, the second two making number 1, or that on their tours they were playing to record numbers of people for up to three and sometimes four hours, carrying the entire show themselves. Never mind that Page and Jones had been involved in some of the biggest-selling music of the 1960s, and that Plant and Bonham had done their time hacking around the Midlands. Sales may not always equate with artistic merit, but the media had never before deemed success and merit to be so exclusive.

Understandably, the band was baffled. Looking at it with considerable hindsight, it's easy to dismiss the critics as tone-deaf dolts who were jealous of success and unable to accept that here was a band who didn't need their help to climb the ladder—ergo, they must be in some way artificial, hyped by their record company like the manufactured Monkees had been before them. What was actually happening, in front of their eyes, was a revolution in both music and the industry.

Throughout rock's history, any sizeable shift in the dominant musical style of the day has been hard to divine at the time and only a certain number of fans and critics alike will have initially seen it. With Led Zeppelin, it just seemed to take a little bit longer to be seen by the media, and it was only after producing four albums that their importance really started to dawn on the music press. It took even longer for them to make an impact on the mainstream media.

The other side of this story is, of course, that, with a few exceptions, the group seldom went out of their way to make the media welcome, and were often petulant and dismissive in interviews. According to biographer Chris Welch, the poor relationship stemmed as much from manager Peter Grant as from the band members themselves. Welch believes that it was one incident that set the whole tone of Led Zeppelin's relationship with the media. At one of its earliest London gigs, at the Marquee, Grant had invited a BBC television crew to film the event. When the crew failed to materialize, Grant was dumbfounded, unable to believe that they would have passed up the chance to film his exciting new band. Such was his immense belief in the group and their ability to take on the world, Welch claims, that the manager held a grudge against the media from that day on. The fact that numerous invited print media journalists had turned up did little to humor Grant, and the seeds of the animosity were sown that night.

Taking their cue from the manager, the band members also took a dim view of the press, often raging against the media for projecting their own interpretations onto the music—for daring to actually think about it rather than blandly accept it as a new sermon from the mount. One particular incident in 1971, which occurred after the riot in Milan that had brought their show to a very abrupt and premature end, showed just how naive Led Zeppelin was when it came to handling the media and playing the PR game.

After returning to their hotel from the ransacked and tear-gassed stadium, the band members were soothing their nerves with beer at the bar. They had just seen what Page described as a war zone—10,000 kids forced to flee from the police by invading the stage and trying to get out of the stadium through the backstage area. "We finally got back to the hotel and collapsed into the bar to try and calm down," Page recalled at the time. "Along comes this reporter, a guy who'd been there and seen the whole thing and knew what happened. There we are, completely emotionally shattered, and he comes up to ask for our comments. We just tore him apart, saying, 'C'mon man, you saw it, now you write it up. Don't ask our opinion. You've got your own.' But he kept on bugging us for a comment, and in the end Bonzo told him to piss off or get a bottle smashed over his head." It seems that, in Led Zeppelin's eyes, it was OK for the press to have opinions, just not opinions about *them*.

The undercurrent of violence was hardly an isolated incident. In 1969 Ellen Sander, a writer for *Life* magazine, joined the band for part of its second U.S. tour. This was the tour during which the infamous "shark episode" took place, and, as Sander noted, the band members seemed barely able to lift themselves anywhere near a level of basic human behavior. On the last night, Sander entered Led Zeppelin's dressing room to thank them for allowing her to travel with them. Road madness had taken its toll, however, and they snapped, attacking her and ripping her clothes. Sanders believed she was about to be gang-raped and that only the physical intervention of Peter Grant, who pulled Bonham and others off her, prevented an even uglier scene. Although the article never appeared in *Life*—Sander refused to write it at the time—it was eventually published in a compendium along with other stories.

Such tales hardly endeared the press to Led Zeppelin, or vice versa, and relations between the two grew worse with each and every album, each and every tour. Neither respected the other. According to the press, Led Zeppelin was an anomalous, contrived, money-making machine that relied only on volume and, according to Sander, a "well-engineered promotional strategy." This in spite of the fact that they did not have an official PR person, and their "strategy," such as it was, centered around whether Grant liked you or not. No matter—according to the media, they were barbarians who would soon enough return to whatever cave they'd crawled out of. According to Led Zeppelin, on the other hand, the press were leeches, misreading everything they did, said, or played, parasitically making money by slagging them off.

Originally, the band was accused of being too bludgeoning, of relying on deafening power. When they extended themselves and showed the other side of their musical personality, they were accused of pandering to fashionable whims and deserting their roots. On *Led Zeppelin IV*, they finally melded both elements of their music into one album, but much of the press was still indifferent, although some were less uncharitable than they had been in the past.

Rolling Stone magazine's review of the album, by Lenny Kaye (who was soon to be the guitarist in the Patti Smith Group and the compiler of the seminal 1960s garage rock compilation *Nuggets*) was as guilty as any of damning with faint praise. Starting off pleasantly enough, claiming that the album was "remarkable for its low-keyed and tasteful subtlety," the writer could no longer contain himself and, after pointing out the problems with the album's three predecessors, put the boot in: "If this thing [*Led Zeppelin IV*] with the semi-metaphysical title isn't quite their best to date, since the very chances that the other albums took meant they would visit some outrageous highs as well as lows, it certainly comes off as their most consistently good." Even on the cusp of saying that here was a band coming to grips with both its songwriting capabilities and musicianship, Kaye couldn't resist having a dig.

This writing was typical of anything *Rolling Stone* published about the band at the time. Mostly, it allowed for small news stories that were more about expressing bafflement as to the success of yet another sold-out tour than providing their readers with any useful information. This constant griping by the magazine did both itself and Led Zeppelin a huge disservice, and it wasn't until 1974 that the band finally appeared on the magazine's cover.

It's a situation that the then-staff of the magazine now seem embarrassed about: all those who were contacted and asked for an interview for this book declined, saying it had always been someone else's call, and "get in touch with so-and-so, it was him." Even in the mid-1980s, *Rolling Stone* was still pursuing a policy of damning the album with faint praise. In the *Rolling Stone Album Guide*, published in 1983, *Led Zeppelin IV* was given a five-star rating and was acknowledged as being the band's finest album, but even then the writer couldn't be unequivocal. While lauding "Stairway to Heaven" as being "to the 1970s what 'Satisfaction' was to the 1960s," the guide still had to have a dig, saying that their debut album was actually probably better and suggesting that only the tide of history gave *Led Zeppelin IV* its cachet.

Led Zeppelin IV did, however, eventually find a new level of admiration among many journalists, and in hindsight, their reservations can be seen as nothing other than tempered enthusiasm. In *New Musical Express*, Roy Carr managed perhaps one of the most astute interpretations of the album. Going through it track by track, he singles out "The Battle of Evermore," "Rock and Roll," and, perhaps more surprisingly, "Four Sticks" for particular praise. "Stairway to Heaven" was called "one of the best tracks by any group this year," while Bonham's drumming was praised and Plant's contribution was recognized as the greatest he had yet made to any of the band's albums. Even the legendary Lester Bangs of *Creem* magazine had slightly warmed to the band by now, although he called the album "far from their best" without bothering to state which he considered better. Yet, when handing out what seems to be unequivocal praise for "When the Levee Breaks," he still complained that it was too long. In possibly the biggest blunder, U.K. magazine *Disc and Music Echo* even got the personnel wrong, claiming that, on "The Battle of Evermore," "Robert plays beautiful guitar."

It wasn't all bad, however. The U.K.'s *Sounds*—traditionally the most "rock" of the big three British music publications of the 1970s and 1980s, alongside *New Musical Express* and *Melody Maker*—staked a claim for *IV* being Led Zeppelin's "best recorded material to date." Again, this was hardly shout-it-from-the-rooftops praise. What these and other reviews of the time shared was a feeling that, if nothing else, here was a band that was due at least some grudging respect—and it was only being given grudgingly.

As *Led Zeppelin IV* was a seismic shift in music, it also eventually became a turning point for the band in the eyes of the press. Although both remained suspicious of each other for years to come, the band were never again dismissed as rip-off artists. In fact, the huge success that *IV* achieved would eventually mean that they were given almost universally good reviews on all of their subsequent albums. Obviously this was, by some, an attempt to make up for less than insightful comments in the preceding years, having finally caught up with what Led Zeppelin fans had known all along: that here was a band pushing forward the boundaries of rock, rewriting white blues, and showing that there was an audience beyond the elitist and cozy world in which journalists would often like to keep it.

Something else had gradually changed as well, though, and that was the journalists themselves. Just as Led Zeppelin had arrived to provide the soundtrack of youth for a new generation, so too a new generation of journalist had slowly arrived on the scene—a generation that was less hung up about the past, and more committed to the present and the future. Gradually, as these journalists—people such as Cameron Crowe, with *Rolling Stone*, and Nick Kent, with *New Musical Express*—grew in stature, so did the media's respect for Led Zeppelin.

As the myth and success of the band blue-skied, *Led Zeppelin IV* attained the legendary status it deserved. Today the album regularly appears in any magazine's or newspaper's list of greatest albums of all time, from *The Times* to *Spin*. Some magazines would be expected to rate Led Zeppelin highly; in 2000, *Guitar World* rated *IV* the second-best album of the millennium behind Jimi Hendrix's *Are You Experienced*, while *Classic Rock* named "Stairway to Heaven" the greatest song of all time. But it also crops up in less likely lists. *The Times*, Britain's most staid and conservative daily newspaper, rated *Led Zeppelin IV* in the Top 20 albums of all time. Even *The Wire*, the egghead magazine that usually concerns itself with the more rarefied end of music—jazz, post-rock and electronica—included the album among its list of most important of all time, although the list was presented in chronological order. *Spin* magazine, which often ties itself in editorial knots trying to be painfully hip, voted Led Zeppelin the third greatest band ever behind the Beatles and, more surprisingly, the Ramones (the list was compiled in 2000, shortly after singer Joey Ramone died, possibly making that rating more about sentiment than true merit).

The overriding impression from such lists is a consistent respect for Led Zeppelin, and its fourth album in particular. This respect is perhaps best summed up by the readers of the U.K.'s Q magazine. Q, which considers itself something of an industry standard, has twice invited its readership to vote for their favorites of all time. Both the 1998 and the 2002 polls, rated *Led Zeppelin IV* in the mid-20s, noting that the album had taken hard rock to a higher ground and elevated Led Zeppelin out of the reach of their rivals.

In the final analysis, however, the press doesn't always get it right and history often makes them into fools. Sales of

22 million copies aside, Led Zeppelin can take comfort in the fact that, although they may have had a rough ride initially, the generations of critics and fans who followed now see them for what they were: true innovators, and an inspiration to virtually every rock band that would follow in their larger-than-life footsteps.

good times, bad times: life after Led Zeppelin IV

Although *Led Zeppelin IV* was without doubt the band's creative peak, it was by no means the end of the Led Zeppelin story. Now indisputably the biggest act in the world, Led Zeppelin was to continue its frenzied career for another eight years before finally coming to a tragic halt in 1980.

To promote the new album, the first task was another U.S. tour. In August, the band started its latest North American campaign in Canada, rather than the usual Los Angeles, anxious to find out how the new songs were going to work. Even so, they didn't immediately let the cat out of the bag. It wasn't until they were back on their "home turf" of L.A. that "Stairway to Heaven" was finally revealed in North America.

"Stairway to Heaven" had already been roadtested on audiences in the U.K., however. It first appeared in the band's set during the "Back to the Clubs" tour that had kicked off in March, 1971 in strife-torn Belfast, Northern Ireland, less than a year before the infamous events of what was to become known as Bloody Sunday. On January 30, 1972, British soldiers fired into a crowd of Catholic protesters, killing 13 and injuring a further 14. Riots and confrontations between Catholic youth and soldiers and police had become regular features of life in the major towns of Northern Ireland, but Bloody Sunday marked a new escalation in the violence that would not be resolved for over three decades.

As a result, few touring bands would venture to Northern Ireland for fear of becoming entangled either in the politics or the violence. Indeed, just prior to Led Zeppelin's visit, numerous bands had canceled, but this was a group who prided themselves on going where others refused to tread. In fact, it would be over six years after Led Zeppelin's performance before another major act from outside Ireland—the highly politicized punk band the Clash—would tour to the city. Even then, the Clash would play only one of the two planned shows after lead singer Joe Strummer received death threats conveyed through a local newspaper.

Perhaps surprisingly, the Led Zeppelin gig passed without incident, but was still remarkable for the fact that it showcased the first ever performance of "Stairway to Heaven." Witness to the show was Chris Welch, then a writer for *Melody Maker* and one of the band's "chosen" journalists, who was often invited on tour with them.

"It was the first time any of us had heard the song," Welch recalls. "I remember the audience being hysterical, as usual, and then this incredibly long, structured piece starts with an acoustic section—I didn't know what it was called at the time. The audience managed to sit quietly and listen to it through the acoustic part and then went hysterical again at the end. But at that point, it was just a new song that was taken on its merits."

Even so, Welch was impressed enough to single out the song after the show. "We were going up the steps to the plane afterward to fly out of Belfast, and I asked what the name of the new song was. They said "Stairway to Heaven," which seemed quite appropriate at that moment as we were climbing into the plane."

Five months later, at the Forum in L.A., it was still eight weeks ahead of the album's release and, again, none of the audience had heard the song before. Already enraptured by the band on stage in front of them, they had just given a standing ovation to a 20-minute version of "Dazed and Confused." Twelve minutes later, the crowd was again on its feet, roaring its approval of this new anthem they hadn't even known about until then. Page recalled the experience as particularly satisfying. "It was such a moment. We all know how difficult it is to hear a song for the first time from a group in concert, and it really hit home. It was a really emotional moment."

Although it was a fair uneventful tour by Led Zeppelin's standards, it was special for one reason—it dovetailed with the band's first ever visit to Japan. Between dates, the group rested for a week in Hawaii, with everyone except Page staying at the Rainbow Hilton. The wives joined their husbands for the vacation and Page, as the only unmarried band member, wanted to carry on as he would anywhere else. But that would have given away the game to the womenfolk, who were constantly being placated and told that no, of course the band didn't behave like other groups on the road, they missed their partners a great deal. They had even taken to supplying false itineraries that didn't list Los Angeles, such was their wives' distrust of the diversions that awaited their husbands there. So Page rented a house away from the Hawaiian hotel and told the roadies not to give his address or number to Plant so that he didn't have to worry about the singer bringing Maureen over to visit.

Arriving in Japan, the band found "Immigrant Song" still at number 1 on the singles chart. Even in conservative, buttoned-down Japan, Led Zeppelin was massive and untouchable, and with the wives safely back in the U.K., the usual naughty behavior resumed. Accompanying the band on the tour was Phil Carson, the head of Atlantic Records in Britain and a firm friend of the band who was always ready to join in the mischief. One night, one of his pillows was knocked out the hotel room window by Plant, and Carson decided to climb out on the ledge to retrieve it. While he was outside the window, dressed only in a bath towel, the band rang security and reported a peeping tom outside their suite.

During the same stay, a drunk and comatose John Paul Jones had the door to his suite hacked down by Richard Cole and John Bonham who were wielding recently acquired samurai swords. Dragging the bass player into the corridor, they set about destroying the rest of the room, chopping the furniture into pieces. Jones slept soundly outside, oblivious to the carnage going on behind the wall. When hotel staff tried to rouse him, he harangued them with some rather choice ancient Saxon words until he realized that he had indeed been asleep in the corridor.

Eventually the marauding behavior became too much for the hotel's management. The final straw came after a heavy, prolonged food fight, whereupon Led Zeppelin and entourage were banned from the Tokyo Hilton for life.

But such measures were hardly going to curb the extreme behavior of the band. One particular incident has become a legend in the Japanese rock industry. Following a benefit gig for victims of the 1945 bombing of Hiroshima, the group boarded the Japanese bullet train for their next engagement. Refreshed with sake and Japanese whiskey, Bonham and Jones decided to douse Page with cold water while he slept in his bunk. Pulling aside the curtain, Jones heaved in the water, only to discover they had the wrong room; it was Peter Grant's, and he didn't take kindly to being awakened in the middle of the night. Grant roared down the corridor and caught hold of Jones. When Cole arrived to find out what the commotion was, Grant took a swing at him, missed, and landed one on Bonham. A staff member from the Japanese record company who was witness to the mayhem was ready to resign on the spot over the loss of face. He thought the band was splitting up before his very eyes, and he wasn't able to do anything about it. Carson had to take him aside and explain, record company man to record company man, that this sort of thing happened all the time. The next morning the band got off the train and carried on as normal, but the newspapers got hold of the incident and splashed it over the front pages. During the gig that night in Osaka, Bonham was feeling dazed and wandered off the stage mid-song. It appears he was still feeling the effect of the mighty punch he had copped from his manager earlier that morning.

Following the tour, Page, Plant, and Cole headed for some time off in the Far East, while the others flew back to England. After a quick tour of the brothels of Bangkok, Plant and Page, who had long harbored a desire to mingle eastern and western music, traveled to Bombay to investigate the possibilities of recording with local musicians. Most of all, though, the vacation demonstrated to Led Zeppelin that, although they were selling more albums and playing bigger gigs than any other band in the world, they were far from being a global concern. One particular incident brought it home more than any other. In their Bangkok hotel was a poster advertising an impending show by Marmalade, a British invasion band best known for its rather thin hit version of the Beatles' "Ob-La-Di, Ob-La-Da," although the band continued to have hits in both the United Kingdom and the United States into the late 1970s. In the same city Plant and Page were followed around by kids shouting "billy boy," accusing them of being gay because of their long hair, and not recognizing them as members of the planet's all-conquering rock group. In fact, other than in Japan, they were barely identified by anyone other than drunk western sailors in whorehouses.

Returning to the United Kingdom, the guitarist and singer reunited with the other members for a month-long home tour that sold out in just 24 hours. The crowning glory of the tour was the band's most spectacular attempt at live performance—two nights at London's Empire Pool, Wembley (near the current Wembley Arena site), for which 19,000 tickets had sold out within an hour. The shows were conceived as an entire evening of rock—an ambitious project for a band that had hitherto prided itself on its no-frills approach, that didn't usually have a support act, and that had just released an album designed to be as anonymous as possible.

Instead, Led Zeppelin employed circus performers and, bizarrely, a pig on a trampoline, to warm up the crowd for their support act, Stone the Crows—the first support act the band had used since their second tour of America. The fact that the band happened to be managed by Peter Grant wasn't entirely coincidental. The shows were so successful that they proved pivotal in finally earning Led Zeppelin the grudging respect of the British music press, who gave such glowing reviews that even the mainstream papers had to take notice.

Now, with the album riding high in the charts and immediate touring duties finally over, Led Zeppelin could take some proper time off, and it wasn't until February 1972 that they all gathered together again. Atlantic was pushing for a quick follow-up album, as always, but the band could easily afford to take their time, and they politely told the record company to back off. Page and Jones both had home studios (Page had sold his boathouse on the Thames and bought a rambling country estate, called Plumpton Place, in the southern county of Sussex) and both worked constantly at finding new riffs, rhythm tracks, and sketches of songs. Plant, meanwhile, busied himself reading about Celtic history (particularly about the border wars between Wales and England), while working on his farm near Kidderminster, Worcestershire, and Bonham drove his cars and his tractors and drank at his local pubs.

Page also had another project. He had been approached by Kenneth Anger, a U.S. underground filmmaker better known today for his landmark book about film industry sleaze, *Hollywood Babylon*. Anger was making a short film called *Lucifer Rising*, the follow-up to his 1967 short *Scorpio Rising*. Anger and Page were in some ways kindred spirits, both having an interest in the occult (Anger would play Lucifer in his new film) and both being particularly drawn to Aleister Crowley. It was probably through Anger that Page hatched the idea to buy Boleskine House, Crowley's old Scottish residence; Anger had once spent a year living in the gloomy house.

Anger, having been outbid by Page for a Crowley manuscript at an auction, approached the guitarist to record the soundtrack for *Lucifer Rising*. Page quickly agreed. It was a match that, on paper, seemed made in heaven (or hell, if you prefer) but the partnership turned sour as Page's work on the soundtrack proceeded extremely slowly. Between his band commitments and what would soon become an escalating drug habit, Page had little time to work on the film, even though he would eventually install Anger in the basement of his Kensington house in London, where all the film-editing equipment from the group's film *The Song Remains the Same* had been set up after the project was initially abandoned.

Shortly before the film's release in 1976, Page had only recorded a series of droning snippets on tape that Anger considered inappropriate, and the film was eventually released with a soundtrack supplied by Bobby Beausoleil, a one-time member of the Manson Family.

Such uncertain, unproductive, and dark days were still some time away, however, when in May the band reassembled at Mick Jagger's Stargroves estate to start recording their fifth album. It was probably the most buoyant time of their career, the hard work having paid off with their spectacular success and the knowledge that in their latest album, *Led Zeppelin IV*, they had scaled unimagined heights of creativity. And they had no reason to believe that their creative peak had been crested. But there was a nagging thought: how do you follow up something as spectacular as "Stairway to Heaven," "When the Levee Breaks," or even "Black Dog"?

Their solution was to take their time and make sure of what they were doing. With a stash of around 20 unreleased, rough tracks recorded over the years, including what Page and Jones had been working on privately in recent months, they were hardly unprepared. But they did want to build the album, not rush themselves into something they weren't happy with just to satisfy the record company's desire to mop up their fans' money. Success had bought them even more time to think and experiment.

Part of the process included a return trip to Bombay for Plant and Page, which had been planned during their visit the previous year and was combined with a tour of Australia and New Zealand. (The tour was to start in Singapore, but when they arrived they weren't allowed into the country, which had strict laws about the length of men's hair as a safeguard against the corrupting influence of the West.) Hooking up with members of the Bombay Symphony Orchestra and raga musicians, the pair recorded versions of "Friends" and "Four Sticks," just to see if the patterns of the two musical cultures could be integrated. Yes, the Beatles had done the whole India trip a few years before, and eastern influences had been appropriated on rock albums throughout the late 1960s, not least by Page himself—but no one had actually gone to these musicians and recorded in their environment. There was never any intention to release the songs, but it is fair to suggest that had the results been anything special they would have come to light at some point. As it was, the fans would have to wait until the sixth album and its centerpiece track, "Kashmir," for a real blossoming of this seed-planting exercise.

One night in Bombay again demonstrated to the pair how little they were known in Asia. Jamming in a club to patrons who had barely heard or seen western musicians before, let alone knew who was playing for them, they were given a bottle of whiskey afterward by the owner. He then offered them another bottle if they came back the next night.

Rock 'n' roll, the duo again realized, was hardly the first area of the music business to indulge in a little exploitation.

Although Stargroves turned out to be no Headley Grange when it came to inspiring the band, they nevertheless wrote much of the album while there, although "The Rain Song" and "Over the Hills and Far Away" had been brought along by Page. Jones already had "No Quarter" well on its way when he arrived. Engineer Eddie Kramer, who had also worked on Led Zeppelin II, recalled it as a particularly happy time: "Everybody in Led Zeppelin was just so confident and happy about what was going on," he explained. "I have a very strong vision of all four of them dancing in single file on the lawn during the first playback of 'Dancing Days,' celebrating this incredible thing they'd just recorded."

What they recorded was Houses of the Holy, a very strange chapter in the Zeppelin canon, and the album that has aged least well. For every lightness of rock touch that distinguishes "Dancing Days" and "Over the Hills and Far Away" there is a clumsy, almost oafish sound in "The Crunge" and "D'Yer Mak'er," while "No Quarter" has all the excesses of progressive rock without any of the tittering at the back.

"The Crunge" and "D'Yer Mak'er" were tributes of a sort, the former to Motown, the latter to reggae and 1950s rock 'n' roll. Apologists contend that those who criticize the tracks fail to see the humor and parodic intent, but in this century they sound like a band dislocated from their roots or, even worse, already too cosseted and removed from the world around them to engage with it in any meaningful way. Reggae was just about to explode around the world: Jimmy Cliff already had four Top 20 singles to his name, while Bob

Marley and the Wailers were living in London and about to release their breakthrough album *Exodus*. And here was the mightiest band in the land, totally patronizing the music for which they professed a genuine appreciation. These two songs have been responsible for more attacks on Led Zeppelin than any others over subsequent years; detractors have been able to point to what sounds like the lack of a single genuine funky bone in their collective body as proof that the band were just lumbering heavy metal buffoons.

But that argument ignores the high points and "Dancing Days," "Over the Hills and Far Away," and "The Song Remains the Same"—a frantic yet contented song about the fact that, no matter how far the band may travel, there is always the constant common denominator of music—sound years ahead of their time. They have stayed fresh in spite of the endless carbon-copy groups that followed in Zeppelin's wake over the next 20 years. Even the slightly self-important "The Rain Song" has the kind of beautiful string arrangements that could make Jimmy Webb weep.

Overall, though, *Houses of the Holy* is a somewhat smug album, the sound of a band a little too pleased with itself to bother trying just that bit harder. Perhaps it was what they had recently lost that lends *Houses of the Holy* this air. The length of time it took to record the album removed the spontaneity that had made *Led Zeppelin IV* so immediate, the rush of urgency that had created "Black Dog" and "Rock and Roll." Some bands are, perhaps, better off working against tight deadlines, and it's undoubtedly the case that Led Zeppelin produced its best work when operating within a very strict time frame.

As always, the path of Led Zeppelin never ran true, and, back in the mixing studio, the band found that the Stargroves tapes were far from what they had expected. The sound was nowhere near as good as it had been at Headley Grange, and it took months of rerecording and mixing before the album sounded the way they wanted. Also, as with *Led Zeppelin IV*, there were problems with the sleeve artwork. Surprisingly, it wasn't the naked children on the front, or even the inside picture of a man holding one of the children aloft as if offering a dawn sacrifice. This was all just to be expected from Led Zeppelin, who had, after all, sold their souls to the Devil. (Anyway, this time the record company knew better than to oppose the band's wish to have no identifying words on the cover.) The problem was something much plainer than that: they couldn't get the colors on the sleeve right. The first attempts made the children look blue from the cold, and endless tinkering with the color balance would contribute to months of delay.

In spite of the wait, the band again headed out on the road in America, on their eighth tour of the country. Another low-key affair by Zeppelin standards, it nevertheless cemented their position as the top-grossing act in the world, even though the Rolling Stones were touring their new album, *Exile on Main Street*, at the same time. As the press fell over themselves to heap praise on the Stones they barely noticed Led Zeppelin, something that truly stuck in the band's craw. Outside of their immediate fans and the industry, few people knew the scale of their achievements, while even their own record company billed the Stones as "The Greatest Rock 'n' Roll Band in the World."

The tour gave rise to two significant moments in Led Zeppelin history: Peter Grant changed the music business's operating procedures yet again, and Jimmy Page put the band in jeopardy by chasing after a 14-year-old girl.

Following the phenomenal success of *Led Zeppelin IV* (which was still selling strongly) and "Stairway to Heaven," (which was slowly growing into its role as a generational anthem), Grant decided that a 50–50 split between band and promoter was no longer a fair deal. If shows by his group were going to gross so much money, why shouldn't they have a bigger cut? The kids were there to see Led Zeppelin, not the promoter. So Grant hired the venues out of his own pocket and employed local promoters to do the leg work, advertising the gigs and making the usual security and backstage arrangements. For this they were offered 10 percent of the takings. When they complained, Grant quietly explained to them that 10 percent of a Led Zeppelin gig was better than 50 percent of nothing, or indeed 50 percent of the takings from most other concerts. It made economic sense to the promoter, Grant got what he thought his band deserved, and everyone was happy. It wasn't rocket science for Grant to do the math: it was just that no one before had ever managed a band big enough to call the shots the way he was able to do. Quite simply, no single act had ever made so much money from touring, and no one before Grant had the cojones to take on the industry and win. Again.

Of course, the tour sold out immediately, even without the promoters advertising the dates. Everything went as smoothly as any Led Zeppelin rampage through the United States could, although this time there were problems with illness and Plant losing his voice, a situation that had previously rarely affected the band. One theory has it that the band's increasing use of cocaine was partially to blame, but it wasn't until the next tour that the drug really took a hold on the group. At any rate, the tour continued. Then they arrived in Los Angeles, and Jimmy met Lori.

Lori Maddox, a young model, had met the band's nominal PR man, B. P. Fallon, earlier that year when he was in L.A. with another group. When Fallon showed her picture to Page, the guitarist was instantly smitten. Arriving in L.A., the band checked into their usual hotel, the Continental Hyatt House (legendarily and almost universally known as the Riot House) and Page sent for Lori, to whom he had introduced himself during a phone call from Texas. Because Page was still supposedly seeing Miss Pamela of the notorious groupie gang the GTOs, Maddox avoided his advances, convinced she would be beaten up by her older rival.

Eventually, after chasing her around L.A., Page at last snared his prey through the charming method of having Richard Cole virtually kidnap her from a club. In spite of Page's caveman tactics, the 14-year-old was also smitten, and during the next three years, they would be together whenever Led Zeppelin was in the United States. Not everyone was so enamored by Maddox's charms, however, and Grant insisted that his guitarist's new paramour be kept hidden from everyone in case word got out that he was seeing a minor. Not even Led Zeppelin was big enough to beat a statutory rape charge, and Grant was, for the first time, genuinely concerned that the behavior of his band could slay his golden goose. He had never discouraged Led Zeppelin from letting off steam on the road and often joined in himself, but this was different. It was just about the most illegal act a band could indulge in. If the press or the authorities got hold of this, it could kill their career stone dead.

Aside from the morality of the situation, even now Maddox describes those years as the "most magical of her life." Being on the arm of the world's hottest guitarist isn't something that happens to everyone, and it gave her a glamorous life. She claims that they were deeply in love, and that Page even squared the relationship with her mother. But the illegality of the romance could have blown up in their faces any day, and it is impossible to imagine such a sustained relationship going unobserved in the media today.

With the U.S. tour over, it was back through Japan to England to finish mixing the new album, and to prepare for the biggest-ever tour of their home isles, which again sold out within a day. Led Zeppelin had an insatiable appetite for the road, however, and another, even bigger tour of the United States was organized, this time to coincide with the release of *Houses of the Holy*. When the album was finally issued on March 23, 1973, it hit the Top 10 in just two weeks, making number 1 just after the tour began in May. There were singles released from the new album, although they hardly fit the A.M. format of most Top 40 stations. "Over the Hills and Far Away" only made it to number 87, and "D'Yer Mak'er" scraped in at the bottom of the Top 20, vindicating Grant's belief that his band was all about albums.

More impressive, and earning the band a great deal more money, was the resurgence of the fourth album, which gradually made its way back into the Top 20, nearly two years after its release. It also showed, yet again, that what the

U.S. public had wanted all along was a single of "Stairway to Heaven," now the most popular song on U.S. radio. And, yet again, it showed just how canny Grant had been in insisting that "Stairway to Heaven" never be a single. On this ninth U.S. tour, "Stairway to Heaven" truly made its mark, every night drawing the biggest response from the huge live audiences. Although always a towering song, now it was *legendary*, and, by some estimates, it was being played somewhere on American radio at almost any time of any given day.

Led Zeppelin was now really hitting its stride. For the next three years, the band would be untouchable as a live act, unbeatable as the highest-drawing bill in the world. Along with this came even wilder excesses. Before the massive success of the fourth album, Led Zeppelin's frolics had been fueled by youthful exuberance—they were kids from a relatively socially-repressed country being let loose in the candy store of America. After years of debasement and wanton indulgence, however, where could they go? How could they keep themselves entertained during the dull moments that dragged on between the massive charges of excitement offered by performing in front of hundreds of thousands of broiling kids, all of whom hung on their every utterance, their every move? They were going to gross $30 million for their latest tour—a figure that made even the United Kingdom's *Financial Times*, the equivalent of the *Wall Street Journal*, sit up and run features on the band. The answer to their boredom, now that they could afford it, was to charter their own jet and really start to get their hands dirty.

Fed up with the hassles of having to go through public airport lounges and the security ruck that inevitably occurred just trying to move the entourage through any public place, Grant decided to move his group around the U.S. by private jet. And not just some little corporate Learjet, either. This was a Boeing 720B. Dubbed the *Starship*, it was decked out as a luxury 40-seat hotel in the sky with its own bedrooms, bars, a Hammond organ for John Paul Jones, marble fake fireplaces, and showers—"A flying fucking gin palace," as Richard Cole would so eloquently put it. It allowed the group to base itself in one city and travel out nightly to their next gig rather than constantly move from one hotel to another. One territory conquered, they would move on and start the nightly commuting again from a new base camp. It wasn't cheap, but it was certainly less exhausting, and they could take their entire circus with them to each gig. At one point during the tour, some rich groupies who were unable to gain immediate access to the *Starship* even hired their own plane to follow the group through the skies.

Even so, journalist Chris Welch, who was invited to travel on the *Starship*, recalls that it wasn't all groupies, booze, and drugs. "Flying with them, it was surprising how quiet and well-behaved it all was. They weren't rioting all the time on a continual hotel-wrecking spree. Robert would be reading *Country Life* magazine, choosing his next country mansion, and Jimmy would spend his free time in each city buying antiques." Being a hugely rich rock star had benefits away from the more physical pleasures of the road.

"I once went with Jimmy and Peter to a flea market looking for antiques," says Welch, "and he [Jimmy] bought a rather large table. When it came time to take it back to England, the airline said that the hold was too full, so they had to buy a seat for it on the commercial flight back to the U.K. The table even had its own ticket made out to Mr. Carson, which of course was Phil Carson, the head of Atlantic in the U.K."

The success of *Led Zeppelin IV* had finally changed everything for the band. Whatever they did, wherever they went, everything was bigger now. Far from the tiny clubs they had frequented as the New Yardbirds, Led Zeppelin was now playing to 33,000 people at a time in arenas such as the Atlanta Braves' stadium. In a classic case of having to be careful about what you wish for, even Page was starting to get uneasy about the scale of events. Sneaking into the empty Braves stadium before the doors opened, he took a look around. "It was quite incredible," he said. "There was all this equipment, more than they'd used at Woodstock, on a huge stage. And I looked around the huge arena and I thought, 'My God, there are just four of us.' It tended to make one feel a bit nervy."

Later on the tour, in Tampa, Florida, upwards of 60,000 fans packed into the local stadium, and police estimated that an incredible 90,000 more milled around outside. This in a town that then had a population of around 500,000. Even in terms of album sales, Led Zeppelin was going where no band had gone before: with *Houses of the Holy* at the top of the album chart and *Led Zeppelin IV* back in the Top 20, they were officially recognized as the biggest-selling act on the planet. In fact, their first five albums were now accounting for over 20 percent of Atlantic Records' total record sales.

In spite of Chris Welch's observations, the mayhem within the Led Zeppelin camp had also increased exponentially, and gradually it took on a darker, more violent aspect. Unbound by airline restrictions, life aboard the *Starship* was freewheeling and Bonham was perpetually in his customary touring state: drunk. Welch claims that the drummer's escalating booze intake was the result of a combination of the musician's ancient enemy, boredom, and two other states of existence seldom associated with Led Zeppelin: fear and nervousness.

"They were all quite nervous before gigs," says Welch, "which is where most of the drinking came from. Rock stars were looked after much better backstage in America than in Britain, where you were lucky to get a cheese sandwich. Bonzo was also afraid of flying, and so he drank to cancel out the nerves, but it got worse in later years, which was a shame, really, because he was a lovely, down-to-earth guy, great company. But if you're sitting there, bored and nervous, with a dustbin of Budweiser sitting in the corner, you're going to try and get through it. For me, going on tour with them for three or four days was exhausting, so doing it month after month, it takes its toll. Also, these guys were still in their mid-20s, and you don't think about the possibility that you might damage yourself by drinking."

Drinking often brought out the worst in Bonham, however. One day, stumbling out of the *Starship*'s main bedroom after passing out in an alcoholic haze, Bonham, wearing just a robe, attacked one of the stewardesses in a manner that left no one in any doubt that a rape would have occurred if he hadn't been pulled off the stricken woman. After the incident calmed down, Cole approached the various press people who were enjoying the hospitality and made clear that similar violence would be visited upon them should details of what had just happened get out.

In New Orleans, the band spent time hanging out with drag queens and hurtling through the Bourbon Street bars. Even John Paul Jones, who was usually absent from such activities, got into serious trouble here, going back to the hotel with a girl called Stephanie. When Peter Grant received a call from the hotel manager telling him that "Mr. Jones is all right and so is his friend," he dispatched Cole to find out what had happened. Cole arrived at the hotel to find Jones's door hacked off its hinges. Inside the room, the bass player and his friend lay unconscious. They had apparently arrived back at the hotel, smoked a joint, and passed out, setting fire to the bed, which led to the fire department being called out. Everyone was discreetly ignoring the fact that Stephanie's penis was hanging out of her knickers.

But this was nothing compared to the marauding to come in Los Angeles. Having taken two entire floors of the Riot House, cricket matches and motorbike races were held in the hallway, entire suites of furniture were tossed out of windows, and a table was deliberately thrown out to destroy a convertible parked below after the owner complained about people throwing drinks into it. One observer, Bob Hart, then a writer for the U.K. tabloid newspaper the *Sun*, claims that most of the havoc was the result of drug use. He described the scenes of what was then known as "looning" in an infamous report that resulted in his being banished from the Zeppelin camp, but it finally brought the band to the attention of the wider British public, which even the sales of *Led Zeppelin IV* had failed to accomplish.

What Hart couldn't print was more interesting than what he could. Years later he described the scene to author Ritchie

Yorke: "We couldn't write about the illegal stuff, but anyway, I was writing about the humor of the situation, and some of it was outrageously funny," he said. "However, we were appalled by much of what we saw." Hart believed that much of the extreme behavior was due to a titanic intake of cocaine by the entire entourage. "There was an English girl who was the coke lady. This was so that nobody else ever carried or touched coke. She would apply the coke with the little finger of her right hand, then follow that up with a sniff of cherry snuff and, as a final touch, she'd dab the nostrils with Dom Perignon 1966."

Hart also claims to have witnessed terrible treatment of girls, mainly by the road crew, who would call up a batch of groupies camped out elsewhere in the hotel, amuse themselves for half an hour or so, and then call security to throw them out, ordering another fresh and willing posse. Although he admits that the girls were predatory in their pursuit of Led Zeppelin, Hart doesn't accept that as an excuse for their mistreatment, and he seems to have been genuinely shocked at the general behavior on that top floor.

The other side of the tour, however, was the music and a consistent level of performance by the band that would leave them exhausted and drained just two-thirds of the way though the 33 dates. The show was stretching up to four hours a night, depending on the health of the ever-frail Page, and the audiences were still baying for more, wound up by the pounding of "Rock and Roll" and "Black Dog," half-hour versions of "Dazed and Confused," the anthemic "Stairway to Heaven," and "Whole Lotta Love," during which Page would play a theremin while dressed like a wizard in a black velvet suit covered in mystical symbols.

Eventually the tour ended in New York City with three nights at Madison Square Garden. On the third night it was discovered that $200,000 of the band's money had been taken from their hotel safe. Led Zeppelin always carried large amounts of cash on tour in case Page wanted to buy a new guitar, or Bonham another car, or they just needed more drugs. Although they wouldn't miss a mere $200,000, the band was still rightly upset that they had been taken advantage of and the awkward position it put them in. As Bonham observed at the time, if they had made a fuss they would have been accused yet again of only being in it for the money, but if they acted as if they didn't care, they would have been accused of being too rich. It was a no-win situation. No one was ever charged with the theft. The main internal suspect as far as the FBI was concerned, Cole, passed a lie detector test. Soon after, one of the hotel staff left his job under a cloud of suspicion, although nothing was ever proven.

With $30 million (minus $200,000) gross takings in the bank, the band returned to the United Kingdom and their respective families in August 1973. Page, however, was mentally and physically shot, so much so that his family tried to convince him to enter a sanitarium, something the guitarist himself wasn't entirely sure was an inappropriate measure. "I was thinking," he told a journalist at the time, "that I should be in either a mental hospital or a monastery. It was like the adrenaline tap wouldn't switch off. I'd stay up for five nights on the trot. It didn't seem to affect my playing, but I'd come off stage and I wasn't leveling off at all. I felt I needed to go somewhere with a padded cell so I could switch off and go loony if I wanted. I was quite serious."

It was time for everyone to stop. Tucked away in the countryside, the only Led Zeppelin business the band had to attend to was filming sequences for their proposed film. The Madison Square Garden shows had been chosen at the last minute as the basis for the movie, but director Joe Massot and Grant, who had always harbored celluloid ambitions, wanted more than just a concert film. Massot and crew visited each band member in turn and filmed them in what would become their "fantasy" sequences.

Plant was filmed reenacting a heroic Celtic battle, and Bonham showed off his prize livestock and cars and went to the pub. Jones read *Jack and the Beanstalk* to his daughter and made a mad nighttime dash on horseback dressed as the Phantom of the Opera before getting bored and telling the crew to go away. Page played his guitar beside Loch Ness before climbing a rocky hill and, standing atop it, holding out a lantern like the Hermit from the sleeve of the fourth album. Even the fifth and sixth members of Led Zeppelin, Grant and Cole, were filmed as 1920s gangsters shooting up a country house. Later in the year, after some of the film had been edited, it was screened for the band. Realizing that the fantasy sequences were, as Grant described them, "the most expensive home movie ever made," and that the concert footage was below par, the whole project was scrapped. The editing machinery that Grant had bought was installed in Page's basement to use on Kenneth Anger's *Lucifer Rising*.

Finally, it came time for rehearsals to begin for the next album. After years of procrastination, Led Zeppelin decided that now was the time to release a double album. To do so, they'd mop up all the tracks they hadn't yet released—

material that dated back as far as those visits to Bron-Y-Aur before the third and fourth albums. Alongside those would be a half-dozen or so new tracks.

Another piece of business needed attention first, however. With the end of Led Zeppelin's initial contract with Atlantic nearing, it was time for the band to take even greater control of their career with the formation of their own label, Swan Song. In the past, separate labels for bands had been vanity deals, allowing groups such as the Rolling Stones or Deep Purple their own imprint within the parent label. Peter Grant, however, had other ideas.

Grant wanted a genuine label to which he could sign other bands, operating as an independent entity within the host, much as Atlantic did within WEA (the letters WEA stood for the three labels that merged to create the recording giant: Warner, Elektra, and Atlantic). Following an all-night negotiation between Grant and Atlantic boss Ahmet Ertegun, the deal for Led Zeppelin's label, Swan Song, was set. Unsurprisingly, it was in the band's favor. Ertegun, a wily negotiator and businessman who was known for his poise and unflappability, was overheard coming out of the meeting muttering, "Peter, you're bleeding me dry."

For Grant, the label deal was another chance to get one over on the music industry. For Led Zeppelin, and Robert Plant in particular, it was a hippie's wet dream, the chance to help other artists. Among the first signings to Swan Song was Maggie Bell, the former singer with Stone the Crows, which had disbanded after Les Harvey, the band's guitarist and Bell's boyfriend, had been fatally electrocuted on stage in 1972. The label also signed the Pretty Things, contemporaries of the Yardbirds in the early 1960s, and Bad Company, whose debut album was to provide the fledgling label with its first number 1 hit.

Freedom guaranteed, Led Zeppelin reassembled at Headley Grange in February 1974 to record the next album. The recording followed a similar pattern to that employed for *Led Zeppelin IV*. In three weeks they managed to record eight basic tracks, some with live vocals, before going back to Olympic Studios in London to finish off and mix the album. *Physical Graffiti* is the closest the band ever came to achieving their quest to join western and eastern influences (at least until Page and Plant performed the *Unledded* version of "The Battle of Evermore.") The sprawling 15 tracks of *Physical Graffiti* range from the down-home rock 'n' roll of "Boogie with Stu," which had been recorded with the Rolling Stones' Ian "Stu" Stewart during the sessions for *Led Zeppelin IV*, to acoustic numbers such as "Bron-Y-Aur," which had its genesis during the band's original stay at the cottage in 1969. Both "In the Light" and the album's centerpiece, "Kashmir," were heavily influenced by Page's and Plant's travels through Morocco and India.

A hulking beast of an album, *Physical Graffiti* has flashes of absolute brilliance including tracks recorded during the *Houses of the Holy* sessions which would have made the previous album far more entertaining had they not been left off. Not least of these was the rollicking song that had lent its name to the fifth album and had just the groove that album so desperately lacked. Inevitably, when *Physical Graffiti* was released in February 1975, almost two years after *Houses of the Holy*, it shot to number 1 in the *Billboard* chart after just two weeks, dragging all previous five albums back onto the charts with it. Like *Houses of the Holy*, however, *Physical Graffiti* lacks the compactness of *Led Zeppelin IV* and suffers because of it. In eight songs, *IV* covered just as much musical scope as *Physical Graffiti* ("Kashmir" aside), while having a far tighter focus in its vision. Led Zeppelin was a victim of its own hubris: had *Physical Graffiti* been pared down to a single album, it may just have eclipsed its much bigger-selling sibling. This may merely be snippy criticism, however: 15 million buyers can't be too far wrong, and *Physical Graffiti* is undoubtedly one of Led Zeppelin's two mightiest albums.

As they had after disappearing for a year between the third and fourth albums, Led Zeppelin had come back bigger than ever. The subsequent U.S. tour was hailed as the most exciting rock show ever performed, and the 120,000 tickets for their astonishing six nights in New York sold out in a day and a half. The following U.K. tour was equally triumphant, and even Britain's mainstream daily press, already primed by Bob Hart's reporting of the "looning" that had gone on two years before, suddenly discovered this "new band," Led Zeppelin, hailing them variously as the "new rock gods" and the "new superstar band."

After just five months of frenzied activity, the band all but disappeared again. This time, however, it wasn't to their country mansions in Britain but abroad, in tax exile to avoid the government taking up to 95 percent of their earnings. Plant and his family headed for Morocco, while Page traveled to Sicily to investigate buying Aleister Crowley's old abbey, which still stood empty after all these years, its internal walls still decorated with diabolical paintings from the Great Beast's time of residence.

Back home, there was speculative press talk of a new Zeppelin album, although the band was far from ready to reconvene. It was a happy period, but it wasn't to last. Robert Plant and his family took a vacation on the Greek island of Rhodes with Jimmy Page's four-year-old daughter Scarlet and her mother and long-term, long-suffering partner of the guitarist, Charlotte Martin. Tragedy nearly struck when Maureen, Plant's wife, skidded and crashed the car in which she was driving the family. Maureen was left unconscious (the singer at first assumed his wife was dead), his children were all injured, and Plant had fractured an elbow and badly damaged an ankle. There were no ambulance services on the island, and they had to flag down a farmer's truck to take them to a local hospital, a facility that hardly gave refuge. "I was lying there," recalled Plant, "in some pain, picking cockroaches off the bed, and there's this drunken soldier beside me singing 'The Ocean' from *Houses of the Holy*."

Complicating matters further, Maureen was indeed dying, in desperate need of an unavailable blood type. Charlotte Martin finally got through to Richard Cole in London and explained the desperate situation. Cole took immediate action, but was unable to persuade Swan Song's accountants to release any funds to charter a jet and get his people out of Greece. Thankfully, Claude Nobs, the "funky Claude" of Deep Purple's "Smoke on the Water" fame and a longtime friend of the band, had enough cash available, and a plane was finally secured to take the stricken families to Rome and eventually London for urgent medical attention. Maureen had a fractured skull, leg, and pelvis, and if it hadn't been for Led Zeppelin's wealth, she would have definitely died in

Rhodes. Although she had to spend weeks in hospital, Plant himself was unable to stay in Britain without surrendering a huge amount of his earnings in taxes, and he relocated to the nearby tax haven of Jersey in the Channel Islands. Grant gathered the rest of the band on the island and they decided to head for California and an unscheduled working vacation while the singer recuperated.

They originally moved back into the Riot House, but were hardly in a riotous mood, and soon relocated to beach houses in Malibu. The band slowly worked on new songs. Rumors of an impending new album and tour were scotched by management, however, to be replaced by rumors of a Led Zeppelin split, more because of the press blackout than any lack of work on their part. In spite of Plant's inability to walk without a cane, in November they moved on to Musicland Studios in Munich, Germany, a decision based on their need to flee the States to avoid taxes. Rehearsals in Hollywood had gone well in spite of the circumstances that had brought them there, and the new lyrics Plant had written had a freshness and vigor about them that he attributed to his recent personal circumstances.

Speaking to New York journalist Lisa Robinson, he said, "I've had time to see. Before I was always bowled over by the impetuousness of everything we did. That was knocked off course. I had to think everything anew, instead of just being allowed to go on with the rampaging. The new lyrics are from that period of contemplation, and full of energy because of that primal fight within me to get back."

Presence, Led Zeppelin's seventh album, stands very much alone in the band's catalog. It was the first since their debut album to be recorded at a single location, and only the third that they had recorded entirely within a studio. But setting *Presence* aside from the other studio albums, *I* and *II*, is a sense of age. The first two albums were youthful splurges by young men bursting with energy and ideas, but that was now tempered by everything they had been through, focused into three intense weeks of spleen venting. This was particularly reflected in Plant's lyrics, which were full of reminiscences of moments in their career, from the cocaine high life to times spent carousing along Bourbon Street and the general moment-to-moment existence that Plant had spoken of to Robinson. Here was a man weighing up his life.

Working 18-hour days in the studio, conveniently located in the basement of their hotel, they had no time to filter and sift the way they had ever since that very first album. There is an urgency and tautness to *Presence* that is the very opposite of the sprawling *Physical Graffiti*, and in fact is the nearest, in terms of focus, that they would ever get to *Led Zeppelin IV*. But there is also a shift in sound. Being entirely studio-based, it has none of the organic feel the band had courted since *Led Zeppelin III*, and none of the light and shade they had originally set out to achieve, as perfected on *IV*. In the harsh, neon-sounding guitars and drums you can already hear the approaching second wave of British metal bands such as Def Leppard and Iron Maiden.

For Page, *Presence* was the most musically fulfilling of all their albums, and it's easy to understand his reasoning. Having such a tight deadline (the studio was only available for three weeks, as the Rolling Stones had already booked it and wouldn't alter their schedule) meant that every moment had to count. Also, the band was unsure that they hadn't somehow passed through some unseen membrane, now that their mortality had for the first time been brought very close to their attention. They were rampaging rock gods (even the press said so now), not introspective singer-songwriters, but the intensity of the recording allowed no time to think about that.

Released in April 1976, *Presence* attracted enormous pre-orders from retailers, racking up the highest advance sales of any album in British history. It went straight to number 1 in the U.K., and, like *Physical Graffiti*, took just two weeks to hit the top spot in the U.S. Enthusiasm for the album soon waned, however, as it lacked a "Stairway to Heaven" or "Kashmir," but the group felt justified that they could still cut it—that in spite of everything, they were still up there.

Page, meanwhile, had been through huge personal upheavals throughout 1974 and 1975. During a visit to his Plumpton Place house by Rolling Stone Ronnie Wood and his then-wife Chrissie, Page went for a walk with the other guitarist's partner and they simply wandered off the grounds to start a new life together. Until then few had been aware the couple were even having an affair. At the same time, one of Page's other girlfriends, Bebe Buell, was on her way to London, under the impression that she was about to marry him. Moving with the former Mrs. Wood into his Kensington home, known as Tower House because of its many strange astrological wall decorations and history of occultist owners, he had a very public falling out with Kenneth Anger over *Lucifer Rising*. In an interview, the film-maker accused Page of blowing away his talent in a haze of narcotics but, although Page was undoubtedly becoming increasingly involved with heroin, he was hardly shying away from work, just from working on Anger's soundtrack. Later in the year, Charlotte Martin, who had moved out of Plumpton when Page walked off with Chrissie Wood, became ill, which led to the couple reuniting, although there were always a number of other women within Page's sights.

This was background noise to what was happening with Led Zeppelin, however, who found themselves unable to tour in support of their new album due to Plant's injuries. They had an ace up their sleeves, however, in the tour film from 1973 that they had shelved. Sacking director Massot from the project, they installed a new director, Peter Clifton, and reedited the footage as best they could. *The Song Remains the Same* premiered in New York on October 19, 1976.

It was an immediate success, and the soundtrack album went platinum in America before it had even gone on sale. By November, the film was screening in nearly 60 cities in the States, and by 1977 it had earned over $9 million at the box office. Although by today's standards the film looks incredibly dated, it struck a chord with Zeppelin's stoner fans. Even today, it is a late night favorite of generations of youth, in spite of its musical shortcomings. Recorded at the strung-out end of their most physically grueling tour, brought about not least because of the band's extracurricular activities, the concerts that make up the footage were recorded at Madison Square Garden while Page had badly injured tendons in his hand. None of that, however, matters to Zeppelin loyalists, who still rate it among their favorite concert films of all time.

Finally, in 1977, Plant announced that he was fit enough to tour again, and in February they embarked, incredibly, on their 10th U.S. sojourn. Music papers around the globe were returning end-of-year polls totally dominated by Led Zeppelin. It seemed they were still the biggest band in the world, a position they had held unchallenged for almost five years. Plant, worried about his ability to perform on an unsteady ankle, quickly had his fears allayed, even as he walked up the stage ramp on the tour's opening night. "I constantly thought about what would happen if the foot couldn't take it," he said at the time. "Yet when I walked up the steps to the stage, all the premonitions and anxieties washed away. I thought, 'Ah, it's been so long!' I loved being back up there. I was a loony again."

The tour moved from triumph to triumph. The gigs featured material the band had seldom played in the States before, including the relatively ancient "The Battle of Evermore." Even so, bad vibes permeated the tour. Peter Grant, unhappy because his wife had recently left him, was in no mood to fulfill his usual role of maintaining high spirits. Also, Page was looking desperately ill even before the tour, and there was now an enormous amount of heroin abuse surrounding the group. Worse was to follow.

In Oakland, John Bonham saw one of promoter Bill Graham's security men shove Grant's young son Warren, and the drummer exacted a heavy dose of Led Zeppelin justice. When Grant heard of the incident, he and Led Zeppelin's head of security, John Bindon, dragged the guard into a trailer and beat him while Richard Cole stood watch outside. The next day Bindon, Bonham, Cole, and Grant were arrested, charged with assault, and released on bail. An already dark mood was turning darker, and when they moved on to New Orleans six days later, it turned jet black.

Checking into their New Orleans hotel, Plant was told that his wife was on the phone from the United Kingdom. Taking the call in his room, Plant emerged two hours later to tell the other members of the band that his five-year-old son, Karac, had died of a respiratory virus. The tour was immediately canceled, and the singer flew home, accompanied by his old friend Bonham. He was met at the airport by his father, who, when asked by the gathered media about the situation, reflected: "All this success and fame, what's it worth? It doesn't mean much when you compare it to the love of a family."

It was, unsurprisingly, the end of Led Zeppelin for the next year-and-a-half. Plant did little except grow fat on beer, and his mood was little improved in September by the news that Bonham had been involved in a car crash that left him with broken ribs. Again the rumors, for the first time possibly justified, of an imminent split surfaced, and were, as usual, repeated alongside painfully contrived stories regarding the reaping of karma and the tragedies all being the result of Page's dancing with the Devil. Some stories had it that Plant was finished with Page, that privately he blamed the guitarist's occult dabblings for his family's repeated misfortunes. Page was particularly distraught by such accusations. Feeling the need to defend himself in interviews, he attacked the media for their tasteless timing in view of his friend's recent loss.

Having recently, finally, sorted out his home studio at Plumpton, Page beavered away in isolation, quietly confident that Plant would return to the band when his period of mourning was over. The group had decided that there wouldn't even be discussion of future Led Zeppelin projects until Plant was ready.

The 1977 end-of-year polls again saw the band sweep the board. It was also revealed that their Oakland gigs had been the highest grossing concerts ever, bringing in $1,322,500 for playing in front of 115,000 people over two nights. The news was tempered by the convictions of Bindon, Bonham, Cole, and Grant on assault charges in the new year, for which they were given suspended sentences and probation of up to two years. Bill Graham, furious at what he considered to be too lenient an outcome, was reported to have commented, "So, they'll never learn."

In May 1978, Led Zeppelin gathered together for the first time since Karac's death and decided to set about a new album. In the intervening months, punk had hit the United Kingdom, its main protagonists railing against the old guard of groups, none more so than Led Zeppelin. The band figured they had something to prove as the press again turned on them. Plant, in particular, was taken with the new musical movement, however, and was often spotted at the back of punk gigs, but he seldom stayed long after being recognized. He was the enemy, after all. In light of the singer's newfound enthusiasm with this primal music that matched the ferocity and intensity of the artists that had first inspired him, it's perhaps surprising, and in no little way disappointing, what the band did next. Instead of taking a lead from punk and returning to their roots, Led Zeppelin retreated to a hi-tech Swedish studio owned by ABBA.

By now, Page's heroin addiction was starting to overtly affect his work, and he became more and more withdrawn, leaving the rest of the band to get on with it. John Paul Jones took over the running of the sessions, and it proved to be the one and only time that most of the tracks on an album would be largely composed by the bass player. Speculation about the heightened role of Jones, who, along with Plant, worked up most of the songs (which were then augmented by Page), has long kept Zeppelin watchers in conversation. The matter was diplomatically dealt with in a 1991 interview that Jones gave to Ritchie Yorke, in which he said that it was just a matter of circumstance: "Robert and I tended to arrive at rehearsals first."

Although flawed, *In Through the Out Door* was a brave album to release at a time when punk ruled the roost. Depending on your point of view, the keyboard-driven blues it contains are either lushly arranged or hideously overblown. Lyrically, this was largely Plant dealing with his tragic loss, rather than reflecting on his life as he had with *Presence*—hence the doom-laden "Carouselambra" and "In the Evening," with its constant and uncomfortable cry of "I'm in pain." Gone forever was the wide-eyed optimism and exuberance of *Led Zeppelin IV*; the band had been through too much in its last years to ever come up with something as whimsical and celebratory as "Going to California" or "Misty Mountain Hop."

What *In Through the Out Door* will be most remembered for, however, is kick-starting a record industry that had been declining in the previous year. With record companies uninterested in signing anything other than new wave acts, the suburban American kids deserted the stores in droves, and it was the new Zeppelin album that brought them back in. Suddenly, rock was back on the agenda, and a new generation of metal acts raised on *Led Zeppelin IV* were immediately snatched up by the record companies, who quickly abandoned their new punk credentials and went back to supplying what the kids, rightly or wrongly, wanted to hear.

Behind the scenes, Grant was working on a plan to bring Led Zeppelin back into the live arena. Although they'd been constantly courted by promoters keen to stage a huge outdoor event in Britain, with Led Zeppelin as the centerpiece, it was only in 1979 that the idea was seriously contemplated by the band. Unsure of Plant's willingness to continue away from his family, which now included a newborn baby boy, Grant first had to convince himself, and then his act, that they were still a serious draw. Playing two comeback shows at Knebworth, a privately owned estate that is now recognized throughout the world as a home of heavy rock events, even the band was surprised when they were greeted on stage by a huge roar from 200,000 British fans who hadn't seen them live on home soil since 1975.

Although it was a triumphant comeback, both *In Through the Out Door* and the Knebworth concerts were to be the last moments of glory for Led Zeppelin. What could have been a new beginning for the band—the same thing that, say, Aerosmith managed in the 1980s well after their supposed "sell-by" date—was again to turn into darkness and tragedy.

Reenergized by the response at Knebworth, the band began making plans for the road. Richard Cole wouldn't be with them, however; he had been sacked from the organization after Grant realized during Knebworth that he was unable to function due to a serious heroin addiction. The former road king soon ended up in an Italian jail for six months on a charge of terrorism (police raided his hotel room and found switchblades, syringes, and drugs—but how that constitutes terrorism remains a mystery). Back home, a 19-year-old "friend of the band" was found dead from a drug overdose at Page's home. Nevertheless, plans for a stripped-down European tour continued. The tour was initially successful, but the band canceled some dates on short notice. Observers noted that Page often looked pale and sweaty on stage, and in Nuremburg, Bonham fell off his drum stool during the performance, a result of his constant abuse of alcohol, cocaine, and heroin. A return to the United States was duly announced, and tickets sold like hotcakes throughout the country. It looked like another grand return for the hardy perennials. On September 25, 1980, they gathered in good spirits for rehearsals at Page's new Windsor home.

On his way to the house, Bonham told his driver to stop at a pub, where he ate two ham rolls and drank several double vodkas. During the initial rehearsal he drank more vodka, and continued in the same vein at a party afterward. When he passed out at around midnight, he was helped to bed by his driver, who propped him on his side with pillows. The next day Bonham failed to make an appearance, and in the middle of the afternoon he was found dead, several hours beyond resuscitation. At 32, the greatest rock drummer of his generation—possibly one of the greatest drummers of all time—was gone. The coroner later ruled the death accidental, noting that Bonham had, in the 24 hours up to his death, drunk roughly "40 measures" of vodka, leading to water-logging of the lungs due to the inhalation of vomit.

From the jaws of victory, a final, crushing defeat. In testament to the closeness of the four musicians, there was never any real discussion about continuing after the loss of their friend and fellow warrior. Distraught, they all retreated from view to deal with their grief, and they have seldom spoken of those terrible days other than to say that once Bonzo was gone, Led Zeppelin was over. To Jones and Page, he was the ultimate drummer who could never be replaced, but he had also been one of Plant's closest friends for over half his life, a sparring partner from the age of 15. Every battle they had waged as a band was now ended, and finally an official statement was released: "The loss of our dear friend, and the deep sense of harmony felt by ourselves and our manager, have led us to decide that we could not continue as we were."

The final chapter in the story of the world's greatest-ever rock 'n' roll band had closed.

bring it on home: the legacy of Led Zeppelin IV

If you dare to fly high, you only have further to fall, and few had flown as high as Led Zeppelin. In the years that followed Bonham's death, the surviving members of Led Zeppelin grew further apart, and, although they would occasionally get back together, the expectation always outweighed the reality. The equilibrium had been forever put out of whack.

In the late 1980s Plant would admit that his relationship with Page had deteriorated over the final years of the band as their concerns and lives diverged. Plant was preoccupied with his family and its seemingly relentless run of bad luck; Page was in a very dark place that mainly centered around the occult and taking drugs.

When Page finally resurfaced properly in 1984 with Bad Company singer Paul Rodgers in the Firm, he would claim that he had spent the previous four years "just sitting at home worrying like mad." In fact, he had rarely picked up a guitar during that time, but said he was always "wanting to play, because that's the only thing I can do in life, but not knowing how to go about it." Plant, meanwhile, had forged a successful solo career and seemed relatively content, even though his marriage to Maureen had finally ended in 1983. Jones was the most reclusive, and he wouldn't venture into the spotlight again until 1985 and a Led Zeppelin reunion at Live Aid, although he wrote the score for Michael Winner's 1984 film *Scream for Help*. Peter Grant followed Page's descent into heavy addiction and would eventually fall out with the band completely.

In the immediate year after John Bonham's death, Led Zeppelin fell a long way indeed. Describing the emotion of the time, Plant would say: "It was one of the most flattening, heartbreaking parts of my life. I had a great, warm, big-hearted friend I haven't got anymore. It was so final. I never even thought about the future of the band or music."

In the press, the talk was of comebacks and auditions for new drummers. Again the stories of karmic revenge for Page's occult dabblings surfaced, without a care for how they would affect the living. For years people had accused Led Zeppelin of being a callous and calculated money-making machine, so how could it be possible that they wouldn't continue with a new member, just as the Rolling Stones had after the death of Brian Jones? Surely they couldn't just stop! They had just proved to their audience and themselves that they were still capable of much more, and even the harshest knockers had given them grudging respect in the previous 12 months. However, the reality was much different. In the darkest days of their lives, the once mighty rock gods just shut down completely.

According to Grant, no auditions for new members ever took place, although he was approached by any number of drummers willing to try and fill Bonham's shoes. There was also corporate pressure from Warner Communications, who now owned their record company, for the group to continue, although Grant went to great lengths in later interviews to stress that Atlantic founder Ahmet Ertegun was only ever supportive of the band's wishes, whatever they might turn out to be. Sadly, it would be left to the legion of Zeppelin clones to carry the band's legacy further.

Perhaps surprisingly, as he was the closest in the band to Bonham, it was Plant who made the first big post-Zeppelin step with his 1983 solo album, *Pictures at Eleven*, featuring Cozy Powell and Phil Collins on drums and old Midlands pal Robbie Bluntstone on guitar. The album was well received and a commercial success, but never withstood the inevitable comparisons that were made with Led Zeppelin. In fairness, it wasn't designed to. It was a step away from the past, however, and was part of the process of finding a future without virtually the only people that Plant had ever recorded with.

While Plant hit the promotional circuit with his album, Page bundled together various Zeppelin offcuts for a final release, *Coda*. Taken from rehearsals, live performances, and tracks that had been left off other albums throughout the years, *Coda* is a hodgepodge of ideas and eras that, like Plant's solo effort, could never live up to expectations. As a clearing of the cupboard, though, it served its purpose and was surprisingly successful, staying on the American charts for just over a year.

Solo projects came and went. Plant recorded a second album, *The Principle of Moments*, and toured. Page occasionally appeared on stage at benefits, and finally teamed up to tour with Bad Company singer Paul Rodgers as the Firm. He also told friends he was quitting smack, admitting that he had been taking the drug every day for the last seven years.

Throughout the 1970s, every rock band in the world had struggled to keep up with or emulate Led Zeppelin. By now there was an entire generation that had been inspired to form bands as much by Led Zeppelin as anyone else. Starting in the mid-1970s, clone groups had begun emerging, some adhering to the Plant/Page blueprint of flamboyant singer paired with enigmatic guitarist, some taking a more direct approach and, ironically, considering the charges that were forever leveled at Led Zeppelin, nicking all their best licks. Some, like Aerosmith, merely copied the lifestyle that Led Zeppelin had helped define. After "Stairway to Heaven," every band involved with heavy metal—a genre that hadn't really existed as such until *Led Zeppelin II*—had to have a big, building ballad on their next album, suddenly realizing that endless thumping riffs simply made them look Neanderthal.

The most obvious parallel acts to Led Zeppelin were Deep Purple and Black Sabbath, the two touchstone bands of heavy metal. Deep Purple started as a very English folk rock band with mystical pretensions and swirling keyboards, but it decided to change its sound after hearing Led Zeppelin's debut. Ironically, Zeppelin's listening tastes weren't a million miles from those of Deep Purple but, as Led Zeppelin's less bluesy influences became ever more obvious, Deep Purple moved the other way, pitching its tent firmly in the heavy rock camp and seldom returning to its earlier sound.

Black Sabbath, meanwhile, was even more crushingly dark, rarely showing any of Led Zeppelin's lightness of touch. By the release of its defining album, 1972's *Vol. 4* (the title itself is an echo of Led Zeppelin's fourth release), the band already knew they had been left standing at the side of road, musically speaking. Interestingly, Sabbath suffered at the hands of critics in a similar fashion to Led Zeppelin, never being taken seriously. While the press would eventually attempt to patch things up with Led Zeppelin, however, no such courtesy would be extended to Black Sabbath until Ozzy Osbourne's belated success as a solo artist and the band's reuinion tours of the mid 1990s.

A third, and some would say third-rate, U.K. metal band of the era that owed it all to Led Zeppelin was Uriah Heep. More than most, Uriah Heep swallowed wholesale the "olde worlde" mysticism that Zeppelin dabbled with, reaching its peak with 1972's *Demons and Wizards*. The album, recorded in the immediate aftermath of *Led Zeppelin IV*, ends with a medley, "Paradise/The Spell." The track builds from an acoustic beginning to swirling organ and ends as a screaming rocker. It was the band's magnum opus. It's fair to assume that, talented though they might be, Uriah Heep would never have come up with their cornerstone song if Led Zeppelin hadn't shown them the way with "Stairway to Heaven."

Even more obvious among the early imitators was Canadian trio Rush, whose self-titled 1974 debut was the Led Zeppelin of "Black Dog," "When the Levee Breaks," and "Whole Lotta Love" from start to end. Later, when drummer Neil Peart joined the group and became its principal songwriter, he dragged the latent progressive-rock tendencies out of the band's former blues approach, echoing "Stairway to Heaven" and, lyrically, "The Battle of Evermore."

Also early on the bandwagon, with a bizarre marriage of the riffing from "Rock and Roll," Plant's screaming "Black Dog" vocals, and Alice Cooper's theatricality, was Kiss, one of the most enduring rock brands of all time. Formed by bass player Gene Simmons and guitarist Paul Stanley, Long Island's Kiss added a dash of U.K. glam rock to the Zeppelin model (Simmons was a fan of Page's as far back as the Yardbirds) when they debuted in 1974. The camp pomp of Plant was unmistakable in Paul Stanley, even if it was buried under cartoon makeup.

As Led Zeppelin begat Kiss, so Kiss begat one of the most successful metal bands of the 1980s, one that was to advance heavy rock nearly as much as Led Zeppelin had before them: Van Halen. Recording their first demos in 1977 with money put up by Gene Simmons, their combination of guitarist Eddie Van Halen and singer David Lee Roth was classic Page/Plant. Van Halen was, like Page, a self-taught guitarist who took the instrument places it had never been before, inventing techniques that were copied by hair metal acts throughout the 1980s and, later, the nu metal bands of the 1990s and beyond. Roth, meanwhile, took Plant's flamboyant posturing to a new level of theatricality, albeit wrapped in layers of irony. The Led Zeppelin influence was there in the titles of their first two albums, *Van Halen* and *Van Halen II*, and when Roth left the group in 1985, the band replaced him with a man who sported Robert Plant's hair: second-division arena rocker, Sammy Hagar.

In 1984 came Page's and Plant's first joint post-Zeppelin project, a studio album by the mysterious Honeydrippers. Gathering a superstar band together—including Jeff Beck and Chic's Nile Rodgers—and convincing Ahmet Ertegun to produce the sessions (under the none-too-codified nom de plume of Nugetre), a collection of 1950s and 1960s R & B songs was released. One of the songs, a crooning version of "Sea of Love," provided Page and Plant with the highest-ever single chart placing of their career. Although the uncredited band was supposed to remain anonymous, their identities were the music industry's worst-kept secrets, and Plant became horrified by the Honeydrippers' commercial success.

"If that was the last thing I ever did—oh dear," Plant said in an interview at the time. "After all those years of "Kashmir" and "Communication Breakdown," suddenly "Sea of Love" is the height of my achievement. God." Plans for a second volume never got off the ground.

Commercial success aside ("Sea of Love" was one of the biggest-selling singles of that year, while both of Plant's solo albums to date sold over a million copies, a figure below which his solo work would never drop), these were still troubled times. A second bust in three years for possession of cocaine saw Page facing a jail sentence, but a lenient judge surprised everyone by letting the guitarist off with a £450 fine. The judge told Page that a custodial sentence, the norm for a second class-A drug offence in the United Kingdom, "may well prevent you from pursuing your profession"— which is, after all, the idea behind punishment. So selling 20 million albums did have its non-monetary uses.

The brush with prison seemed to shake Page out of his torpor, however, spurring him on to getting the Firm back together and touring North America. During the tour, Page made himself available to the press for interviews, candidly admitting that he and Plant weren't on speaking terms anymore, a situation that would continue off and on to the present day. He dismissed the idea of them ever playing together again. Time has a funny way of making people eat their words, however, and in 1985 a proper Led Zeppelin reunion finally took place.

Live Aid was arguably the biggest musical happening of all time, a global event that established the roots of today's celebrity culture. For one day, rock music was no longer about rebellion: it was about conscience and doing the right thing, raising millions around the world for famine relief. Two simultaneous concerts were to take place in London and Philadelphia, the stars of the day each taking a 20-minute slot in front of packed stadiums and televised to millions around the world. Plant had been unable to join the recording of the charity song "Do They Know It's Christmas" and was keen to take part in the concert. He was already touring America supporting his third solo album *Shaken 'n' Stirred*, but Phil Carson—once the head of Atlantic Records in Europe and now manager to both Plant and Page—brokered a much better gig for the Live Aid producers, reuniting all three of the surviving members of the second-biggest group the world had ever known. With Jones on keyboards (his first appearance since Bonham's death), Tony Thompson of Chic and Phil Collins on drums, and Paul Martinez from Plant's touring band on bass, Led Zeppelin took to a stage for the first time in five years.

Sadly, it was not a success. After two hours of rehearsals in the afternoon, the group played three songs—"Rock and Roll," "Whole Lotta Love," and "Stairway to Heaven"—but they sounded awful. Page's guitar was out of tune, and Plant's voice was hoarse from the rehearsal and his recent gigs. Live Aid was a career stepping stone for many of the participants and it revived the fortunes of others, but for Led Zeppelin it only brought deflation. Plant felt it more than anyone; he had, after all, established himself as a successful solo artist. "The people around us were congratulating themselves for being there because that's what they'd always wanted," he said of the experience. "Yet there are a lot more important things to want than Page and I staggering around in Philadelphia, me hoarse and him out of tune. It smacked of the shambles and shoddiness that Led Zeppelin could never get away with." In spite of the reunion, the members of Led Zeppelin were further apart now than they had ever been.

When you've lost your way, however, sometimes the only place to go is back where you came from. The following year Page, Plant, Jones, and Tony Thompson gathered in a village hall near Bath, England and started rehearsing. Plant had recently split up his touring band and Page had dismantled the Firm, but they had no new material between them and just jammed around. When Thompson was involved in a car crash, a drum roadie took over his stool, but the spirit of the venture soon disintegrated. In the evenings, Plant and Jones would go for a pint in the local pub, but Page refused to join them, which irked the singer, who was the first to crack.

"The whole thing dematerialized: no proper drummer, Jimmy having to change the battery on his wah-wah pedal every song-and-a-half. And I said, 'I'm going home.' Jonesy said, 'Why?' 'Because I can't put up with this.' 'But you put up with it before.' And I said, 'Look, man, I don't need the money, I'm off.' For it to succeed in Bath, I would need to have been more patient than I had been in years." Plant was also confiding to friends that perhaps certain members of the band weren't really in good enough physical shape to measure up to the job.

Plant's fourth solo album, 1988's *Now and Zen*, was finally a turning point for the singer. Having given Led Zeppelin's legacy a relatively wide berth for years, he was now at ease with his past and was willing to embrace it. Inviting Page to play on two tracks, he also used samples from "Whole Lotta Love" and "Black Dog," something that bemused his old partner. "Jimmy was like, 'What is he doing? Is he taking the piss out of it?'" Plant said at the time. "I'm not taking the piss, I'm showing the world that his riffs are the mightiest the world has ever heard." On the tour for the album, Plant started including Led Zeppelin songs in his shows for the first time, although "Stairway to Heaven" was never going to be one of them. "Misty Mountain Hop" was the only track from *Led Zeppelin IV* that snuck under the radar.

Part of Plant's softening to his past was no doubt due to the musical climate of the time. Nearly a decade after Led Zeppelin's last meaningful contribution as a band, rock was again being taken seriously. Although the lifestyle that Led Zeppelin pioneered was never far from the surface of even the most "serious" 1980s indie act (face it, who in a band could resist even the smallest bit of rock 'n' roll behavior from time to time?), their rock posturing was still viewed with suspicion by the sons and daughters of punk. However, occasionally a band would poke its head over the parapet and admit that maybe Led Zeppelin's musical legacy did have something to offer.

Bands who kept the metal flame burning during the 1980s, such as Iron Maiden, Def Leppard, Judas Priest, WASP, Bon

Jovi, and Whitesnake, all owed much of the groundwork for their music to Led Zeppelin—most specifically to *Led Zeppelin II* and the softened rock edges of *Led Zeppelin IV*—but few owed quite as much as the Cult. Borrowing Jimmy Page's guitar orchestrations, the Cult's two main protagonists, singer Ian Astbury and guitarist Billy Duffy, eventually shed their goth-tinged beginnings and reinvented themselves as a straightforward, heads-down metal act, releasing the heaviest album of their career, *Electric*, in 1987. The Cult was nothing if not canny and chose as producer Rick Rubin, the man who the year before had enjoyed enormous worldwide success inventing white rap by marrying "When the Levee Breaks" to the Beastie Boys. *Electric* took the basic rock elements of *Led Zeppelin II* and *IV* and amped them up into a cartoon version of their heroes, both on and off the stage. But the band was not to be a long-lived success, and falling sales in the early 1990s eventually saw them lose their third drummer, Matt Sorum, to the band that would realize everything the Cult had wished for: Guns N' Roses.

When Guns N' Roses released its debut album, *Appetite for Destruction*, in 1987, it seemed to many to be the second coming. Here, finally, was a band as hard, bad, and dangerous as Led Zeppelin had been in its absolute prime. Musically, too, it was a band who had more than just a little of Led Zeppelin's talent. Alongside the hard rock of "Welcome to the Jungle" was a sensitivity and delicacy, as reflected in its breakthrough single "Sweet Child O' Mine." As a band, the members also presented themselves very much in the mold of Led Zeppelin: a screeching blond singer with the now de rigueur camp Plant moves, partnered by a dark and mysterious guitarist who played a Sunburst Gibson Les Paul, all the while nonchalantly dangling a cigarette from his lips. They even had a rhythm section that swung in a way no stodgy rock band had managed since "Misty Mountain Hop." Teenaged boys and groupies flocked to them like they had to no one since Led Zeppelin.

It was in this climate that Led Zeppelin decided to reform for a one-off performance at the 40th anniversary of Atlantic Records, this time with Bonham's son, Jason, playing drums. From the moment he could sit on a stool, the young Bonham had been encouraged by his father to hit drums, and consequently much of his father's style rubbed off on him. In fact, so impressive was his playing that Phil Carson was able to set the youngster up with his own recording contract that day.

Even so, reports of the performance were varied, ranging from "stellar" (Carson, then their manager) to "diabolical, the worst thing they've done" (Peter Grant, now very much their ex-manager). The truth of the matter was that Page was at best indifferent during the performance, and at worst difficult off the stage (he had insisted Atlantic rent the hotel suite beside his as well, because the ringing of its telephone annoyed him).

Again, it wasn't enough to encourage a permanent reunion, and soon after the gig, Page's first solo rock album (albeit featuring Plant's vocals on one track, which was also their first writing collaboration in nearly 10 years) hit the shelves. Carson had set up a record deal for Page with Geffen Records but, two days before it was due to be signed, Page sacked Carson as manager. Rather than be diplomatic about the incident, Carson made his displeasure known in subsequent interviews, claiming that the guitarist was in dire need of sorting out his personal life and letting someone get close enough to him to help him straighten it, and himself, out.

The album barely registered with anyone but diehard fans, and the members of Zeppelin pussyfooted around each other. Page and Plant occasionally joined each other on stage—or not, as was nearly the case when Led Zeppelin was inducted into the Rock and Roll Hall of Fame in 1995. Although all three members were present, skulking around the room, they were rumored to be unlikely to take the stage because they couldn't agree on which drummer to use. Eventually they spent some time jamming with Steven Tyler and Joe Perry from Aerosmith and, later, with Neil Young.

Relations between the singer and the guitarist had hit rock bottom some two years before, in 1993 when, yet again, rumors of a reunion album and tour were in the air. Plant hadn't worked with a band for over a year and Page too was restless, but something about dredging up the past made the singer pause. In frustration, Page turned to an unlikely partner: David Coverdale.

Coverdale had been a complete unknown when he was chosen to front Deep Purple after its most successful vocalist, Ian Gillan, left the band in 1973. Very much a rock belter in a style somewhere between Gillan and Plant, he could imitate either spectacularly. After leaving Deep Purple and attempting a brief solo career, he formed Whitesnake, the best of the Zeppelin clone bands, but one that ultimately embraced the pomposity that Led Zeppelin had somehow managed to steer clear of. In 1987, Whitesnake released "Still of the Night," one in a chain of Zeppelin rip-off singles that sounded so close to the original as to be imitation rather than flattery.

The album that resulted from Page's and Coverdale's collaboration is probably the closest that any former member of Led Zeppelin has come to emulating their old band. Simply called Coverdale/Page (the title referred to neither the name of the act nor the album, keeping it as generic as possible, letting the music do the talking . . . sound familiar?), it does nothing so much as recall Led Zeppelin's heyday. For the aggression of "Easy Does It" and "Absolution Blues" read "Black Dog," and for the rollicking "Feeling Hot" see "Rock and Roll." The acoustic intros to "Pride and Joy" and "Easy Does It" aren't dissimilar to those of "The Battle of Evermore," "Going to California," and even the 12-string section of "Stairway to Heaven." "Pride and Joy" and "Shake My Tree," particularly, manage to span most of Led Zeppelin's career between them. Ultimately, though, the album manages to fall between the twin chairs of Led Zeppelin's Chesterfield and Whitesnake's rather clumsy three-legged milking stool.

Plant always avoided direct questions about the project, preferring only to offer the comment that "sometimes Jimmy has a very dark sense of humor." He was, however, heard to refer rather disparagingly to Coverdale as "David Cover-version."

Page and Plant couldn't stay away from each other, however, and they managed to record the ambitious *Unledded* project for MTV in August 1994, combining their long-held love of Arabic music with old Zeppelin numbers. The program aired in the fall and was accompanied by an album and tour.

Meanwhile, John Paul Jones had been slowly working away in the music industry background, mainly as a producer, most notably with British goth rockers and contemporaries of the Cult, the Mission, on their second album, *Children*. Throughout the 1980s, Jones was approached by any number of rock bands to sit in the producer's chair, but these requests were largely turned down. According to Jones, most of these bands wanted to be "Zeppelinized," and the thought of spending months "listening to that sort of music coming through the studio monitors is really a very simple test that most don't pass."

Jones had also been the instigator of the four-CD Led Zeppelin boxed set that had appeared in at the beginning of the 1990s. It was a monumental undertaking carried through and remastered by Page after tracking down the original master tapes of all their studio albums. Surprisingly, many of the originals had been misplaced, and months were spent hunting for them rather than making do with the second or third generation tapes, as they had when remastering the albums for initial CD release in the 1980s.

The turn of the 1990s also saw one of the last flowerings of Led Zeppelin's influence. In Seattle, a new type of rock was being spawned, one that mixed the light and dark stylings of *Led Zeppelin IV* with the politically and socially aware lyrical themes of punk. Grunge finally killed off the last remnants of the heavy metal that Led Zeppelin had virtually invented, and it introduced a new kind of sonically dynamic rock, taking Jimmy Page's ideas into a modern era that would eventually give way to nu metal. This lineage was carried through to today by two bands in particular: Soundgarden and Rage Against the Machine.

Although more closely related to Black Sabbath, Soundgarden still had an extra gear that Sabbath never quite managed—the ability to deliver power without volume—and, in Chris Cornell, they had a singer who took much of his phrasing from Robert Plant. Rage Against the Machine, however, was much more politically motivated, and in spite of being credited with popularizing, if not inventing, the rock/rap hybrid that dominated much of the metal scene through the mid- and late 1990s, it was the riffing of guitarist Tom Morello that truly made the band stand out. While at college, Morello taught himself to play guitar by listening to Led Zeppelin, a debt he would later pay back when he appeared on the Jimmy Page/Puff Daddy track "Come With Me" (the theme song of the movie *Godzilla*), which was based on "Kashmir."

When RATM singer Zack de la Rocha left the band, Rick Rubin, his ear forever tuned to Led Zeppelin's heritage, suggested to the group that they join forces with Cornell and, as Audioslave, they released their debut, self-titled, and heavily Zeppelinized debut album at the end of 2002.

It's not just in rock that Led Zeppelin's influence spread, however, and the band's songs have often appeared in the strangest of places. In 1997, the London Philharmonic released an album of classical versions of Led Zeppelin songs, including "The Battle of Evermore," "Stairway to Heaven," "When the Levee Breaks," and "Going to California." The album was arranged by former Killing Joke members Youth and Jaz Coleman (who is now the in-house composer for the New Zealand Symphony Orchestra).

Although the pieces are interesting enough in themselves, neither fans of rock nor classical music will probably find much in the album to satisfy them.

In 2000, a bluegrass tribute album to Led Zeppelin was released, featuring five of *Led Zeppelin IV's* eight songs: "Black Dog," "Rock and Roll," "Going to California," and, inevitably, "The Battle of Evermore" and "Stairway to Heaven."

But two of the strangest "Stairway to Heaven" covers have come from perhaps the least likely sources imaginable: ancient Christian singer, sweater wearer, and grandfather of 15, Pat Boone, and Australian painter, TV presenter, and occasional novelty singer, Rolf Harris.

In 1997 Pat Boone, best known for his crooning ways and wholesome family entertainment, released *In a Metal Mood: No More Mr. Nice Guy*, an album that pictured him on the front wearing a leather waistcoat, an earring, and a fake tattoo. The last track on the album was a nightclub version of "Stairway to Heaven." Because of Led Zeppelin's supposed association with backmasking and satanic messages, the song almost cost him his Christian audience. Boone believed that his audience would see the funny side of someone like him performing "Smoke on the Water" and, indeed, Alice Cooper's "No More Mr. Nice Guy," but he was attacked by fundamentalist Christian intellectuals for his cover of "Stairway to Heaven," who decried it as being "needlessly offensive to Christians." They also attacked Boone's "naivety about the power of symbols." Can anybody else hear Aleister Crowley laughing from his grave?

Rolf Harris's version, however, is possibly one of the most charming stories in music. An institution in both Australia and his adopted home of the United Kingdom—where he has presented numerous TV shows, from *Rolf's Cartoon Club*, which explained to kids the genius behind classic cartoons, to *Animal Hospital*, in which he reports on sick and injured animals from a veterinary practice—Harris has had an on–off recording career since the early 1960s. One of his singles, "Two Little Boys," was former U.K. Prime Minister Margaret Thatcher's favorite tune of all time.

In 1990, long after he had all but given up musical performance, an Australian comedy show invited Harris to perform "Stairway to Heaven" (they had a different artist perform the song each week). The venerable entertainer told the producer he had never heard of it. Unbelievable as that may be, he still agreed, and requested the sheet music, not wanting to hear the original in case it interfered with his version. In his autobiography, Harris writes that he was unable to make head nor tail of some of the lyric and so "left out the verse about fairies bustling in hedgerows," and duly performed the song with all his musical trademarks, including breathless delivery, a wobble board to hold down the rhythm, and a didgeridoo solo.

In 1993, the TV show released an album that compiled all the versions of the song that had been performed during the show's three seasons. A copy of the album made its way to the United Kingdom, DJs picked up on Harris's version, and eventually the single climbed to U.K. number 4. Not everyone enjoyed it, however; various commentators suggested that it was blasphemous or that Led Zeppelin should sue, but it started a new musical career for Harris at age 63, and he is still touring Australia, Europe, and the United Kingdom today.

After the song had peaked in the charts, one of Harris's aides took him aside and played him the original. Harris's reaction was priceless. "I thought, 'Oh my God, what have I done?,' feeling a mixture of embarrassment and disbelief. I'm very glad I didn't ask to hear the Led Zeppelin recording before I agreed to do the song. Otherwise I would have said, 'No way, you can't muck about with a song like that!'"

In 1995, Peter Grant died of a heart attack. Shattered after Bonham's death, both by grief and drug abuse, he never returned to management, and spent most of his time post addiction with his family and enjoying his large collection of classic cars. Although there had been talk during his lifetime of making a movie based on his life, produced by former Sex Pistols manager Malcolm McLaren, the project was dropped when U.S. film companies showed little interest.

The success of the *Unledded* album moved Page and Plant to record together again with 1998's *Walking into Clarksdale*. Stripping away the Egyptian and Moroccan musicians, they concentrated on a basic four-piece structure; in other words, Led Zeppelin in all but name. It was the first time in 19 years that Plant and Page had written an entire album together. It was also the first time the two had collaborated fully, together, with an outside producer, Steve Albini. Albini, a successful musician in his own right with bands such as Big Black, Rapeman, and Shellac, has also produced many alternative rock acts, including Nirvana, Bush, and Pixies. The result was a thoroughly modern album of old-school intensity, and one that put the duo firmly back on the musical map.

Maybe it was the timing, a sense of enough water having passed under the bridge, that brought it about, or maybe it was the exorcising of Led Zeppelin with *Unledded*, but *Walking into Clarksdale* proved there really was life left in the old dogs.

Nothing has followed since, but, while there are always the rumors that Page and Plant aren't talking to each other again on any given week, never give up hope that maybe, just maybe, they might even remember John Paul Jones's phone number next time.

The history of the former members of Led Zeppelin and Peter Grant, after the death of Bonham, is one of moving on and trying to achieve great things, but never quite being able to shake off or measure up to the past, particularly those two weeks spent at Headley Grange in 1971.

Together, Jimmy Page, Robert Plant, John Paul Jones, and John Henry Bonham were somehow much, much more than the sum of their parts, as opposed to contemporaries like, say, Deep Purple, who were very much only the sum of their parts. Their body of work, from the faltering blues bluster of *Led Zeppelin* to the unwieldy but gloriously gonzo synth rock of *In Through the Out Door* stands mightier than almost any other, as relevant a blueprint for any band starting today as ever. And standing mightier than them all is *Led Zeppelin IV*, the sleekest, nastiest, most beautifully affirming and supreme rock album of all time. Even Rolf Harris agrees.

bibliography

Cole, Richard with Trubo, Richard. *Stairway to Heaven: Led Zeppelin Uncensored*. Harper Entertainment, 2002.

Davis, Stephen. *Hammer of the Gods: The Led Zeppelin Saga*. William Morrow, 1985.

Godwin, Robert. *The Making of Led Zeppelin's IV*. Collectors Guide Publishing, 1997.

Godwin, Robert. *Led Zeppelin: The Press Reports*. Collectors Guide Publishing, 1998.

Harris, Rolf. *Can You Tell What It Is Yet? The Autobiography of Rolf Harris*. Corgi, 2002.

Hoskyns, Barney. *Waiting for the Sun: Strange Days, Weird Scenes, and the Sound of Los Angeles*. Bloomsbury, 1996.

Napier-Bell, Simon. *Black Vinyl, White Powder*. Ebury, 2001.

Welch, Chris. *Peter Grant: The Man Who Led Zeppelin*. Omnibus, 2003.

Yorke, Ritchie. *Led Zeppelin: From Early Days to Page and Plant*. Barnes and Noble, 1975. (Updated edition published by Virgin Books, 1999.)

index